BUILDING BETTER BOUNDARIES: A 52-WEEK DEVOTIONAL

Building Better Boundaries

A 52-WEEK DEVOTIONAL

Devotions and Faith-Guided Wisdom to Help
You Develop Healthy Relationships

Alexis Waid

ROCKRIDGE
PRESS

Copyright © 2022 by Rockridge Press, Oakland, California

No part of this publication may be reproduced, stored in a retrieval system, or transmitted in any form or by any means, electronic, mechanical, photocopying, recording, scanning, or otherwise, except as permitted under Sections 107 or 108 of the 1976 United States Copyright Act, without the prior written permission of the Publisher. Requests to the Publisher for permission should be addressed to the Permissions Department, Rockridge Press, 1955 Broadway, Suite 740, Oakland, CA 94612.

Limit of Liability/Disclaimer of Warranty: The Publisher and the author make no representations or warranties with respect to the accuracy or completeness of the contents of this work and specifically disclaim all warranties, including without limitation warranties of fitness for a particular purpose. No warranty may be created or extended by sales or promotional materials. The advice and strategies contained herein may not be suitable for every situation. This work is sold with the understanding that the Publisher is not engaged in rendering medical, legal, or other professional advice or services. If professional assistance is required, the services of a competent professional person should be sought. Neither the Publisher nor the author shall be liable for damages arising herefrom. The fact that an individual, organization, or website is referred to in this work as a citation and/or potential source of further information does not mean that the author or the Publisher endorses the information the individual, organization, or website may provide or recommendations they/it may make. Further, readers should be aware that websites listed in this work may have changed or disappeared between when this work was written and when it is read.

For general information on our other products and services or to obtain technical support, please contact our Customer Care Department within the United States at (866) 744-2665, or outside the United States at (510) 253-0500.

Rockridge Press publishes its books in a variety of electronic and print formats. Some content that appears in print may not be available in electronic books, and vice versa.

TRADEMARKS: Rockridge Press and the Rockridge Press logo are trademarks or registered trademarks of Callisto Media Inc. and/or its affiliates, in the United States and other countries, and may not be used without written permission. All other trademarks are the property of their respective owners. Rockridge Press is not associated with any product or vendor mentioned in this book.

Interior and Cover Designer: Lisa Forde
Art Producer: Maya Melenchuk
Editor: Adrian Potts
Production Editor: Dylan Julian
Production Manager: Martin Worthington

Scripture quotations are from THE HOLY BIBLE, NEW INTERNATIONAL VERSION®, NIV® Copyright © 1973, 1978, 1984, 2011 by Biblica, Inc.® Used by permission. All rights reserved worldwide.

Paperback ISBN: 978-1-63878-115-8 | eBook ISBN: 978-1-63878-275-9
R0

**TO MY BEST FRIEND
AND HUSBAND, AARON,**
who taught me what boundaries
and love really look like and who is my
biggest supporter. None of this
would have been possible without
your love and support.

Contents

INTRODUCTION x

HOW TO USE THIS DEVOTIONAL xii

TRUST IN GOD FOR GUIDANCE xiv

WEEK 1
What Is Healthy? 2

WEEK 2
Even Jesus Set Boundaries 4

WEEK 3
Your Foundation for Boundaries 6

WEEK 4
Do You Have a Plan? 8

WEEK 5
How to Say No 10

WEEK 6
When to Say Yes 12

WEEK 7
How Much Time Are You Giving to Yourself? 14

WEEK 8
Relationships Are Hard 16

WEEK 9
Do You Have Clear Expectations? 18

WEEK 10
Prayer Is a Way to Help 20

WEEK 11
Are You a People Pleaser? 22

WEEK 12
Who Do You Need to Forgive? 24

WEEK 13
Finding Your Voice 26

CHECK IN WITH THE LORD 28

WEEK 14
Time Management 30

WEEK 15
Don't Let Others Steal Your Confidence in God 32

WEEK 16
When to Walk Away 34

WEEK 17
You Are Worthy 36

WEEK 18
Are You Out of Balance? 38

WEEK 19
Are You Too Available? 40

WEEK 20
Break Through the Excuses 42

WEEK 21
Hidden Motivators 44

WEEK 22
Have a Different Perspective 46

WEEK 23
You Aren't Supposed to Carry It All 48

WEEK 24
Seeing What's Really Important 50

WEEK 25
Put Your Own Oxygen Mask on First 52

WEEK 26
The Call Not to Worry 54

CHECK IN WITH THE LORD 56

WEEK 27
Procrastination 58

WEEK 28
Dealing with Difficult People 60

WEEK 29
Handling Criticism 62

WEEK 30
Don't Be Too Quick to Respond 64

WEEK 31
How to Stick to Your Guns 66

WEEK 32
Let Others Also Take Responsibility 68

WEEK 33
Is the Argument Worth It? 70

WEEK 34
Identifying Your Triggers 72

WEEK 35
You Are Only Responsible for Yourself 74

WEEK 36
Meet Problems Proactively 76

WEEK 37
Stop Trying to Win People Over 78

WEEK 38
Breaking the Cycle 80

WEEK 39
Dealing with Harsh Words 82

CHECK IN WITH THE LORD 84

WEEK 40
Facing Reality 86

WEEK 41
Don't Accept Others' Bad Behavior 88

WEEK 42
Online Boundaries 90

WEEK 43
Are You Being Authentic Online? 92

WEEK 44
Workplace Boundaries 94

WEEK 45
Church Boundaries 96

WEEK 46
Be Mindful of What You Consume 98

WEEK 47
Toxic Relationships 100

WEEK 48
The Damage of Gossip 102

WEEK 49
The Complaining Trap 104

WEEK 50
The Temptation of Instant Gratification 106

WEEK 51
Avoiding Anger 108

WEEK 52
Embody Self-Control 110

CHECK IN WITH THE LORD 112

MOVING FORWARD WITH YOUR BOUNDARIES 115

INDEX 116

Introduction

Boundaries do not come easily for a lot of people. When I began my career as a youth minister, I quickly learned that I was one of those people. While I was successful at protecting my time and energy so I could remain focused on my work, I struggled profoundly with taking on personal responsibility for the decisions and beliefs of the teenagers I was serving. Their problems became my problems, and their struggles weighed heavily upon me. When my teens struggled in their faith or left my youth group, no matter the reason, I felt crushed. It was also around this time that I began to realize this same pattern had always been there in my personal relationships with friends and family. I couldn't help but become overly involved in the issues of others.

After years of struggling with my own unbalanced boundaries, I began seeking a deeper understanding of the topic. My studies in Christian spiritual formation, soul care, and discipleship at seminary established a working foundation for me of healthy boundaries. Learning to implement them took time and hard work, but I was eventually successful at creating and maintaining boundaries in my life.

So many Christians struggle with boundaries, particularly when they confuse the message of Christ with the idea that they need to be everything to everyone. In this devotional, we will pay particular attention to how Jesus thought about and used boundaries to help you better understand what He is calling you to do in your life right now.

Before we continue, let's establish a working definition of boundaries so we are all on the same page. Boundaries are intentional limitations you set that enable you to peacefully navigate decisions, options, and obligations in your life. Purposeful boundaries are necessary to fulfill your God-given calling to follow in the steps of Jesus Christ.

This devotional will guide you through 52 weeks of thoughts, reflections, and calls to prayer that will help you better understand, process, and apply boundaries in your life. Completing this devotional will equip you with a wide array of thoughts and practical ideas for establishing healthy boundaries—all based in the wisdom and teaching of the Bible. The purpose is to help you build a toolbox within yourself to understand, set, and maintain the boundaries you need in your life right now, and give you the tools you need to establish healthy boundaries in the future.

Setting boundaries isn't easy, but it will lead you away from acting out of obligation and guilt and toward authentically loving and caring for others. Recognizing your own limitations will ultimately free you to make better choices and be able to do the things you genuinely want to do. More importantly, boundaries will liberate you to act on the things God calls you to do.

Finally, while God is the great healer and restorer of all things, God also equipped humanity with skills and careers that help bring about health. Sometimes setting boundaries and getting healthier are best accomplished through the work of a licensed therapist—which I am not. If you feel overwhelmed by the circumstances that led you to pick up this devotional, please consider the help of a reputable therapist who can personally lead you in navigating the issues weighing upon you.

How to Use This Devotional

The intention behind this devotional is that you will use it once a week for a full year. Each week begins with a Bible verse to help you center on God's Word. It is followed by a devotion based on the Scripture for the week that will help you create healthy boundaries in your life. Boundaries are not simple, black-and-white lines, but are complex, varied, and multilayered, so the devotions will address many different topics that will help you create healthy boundaries in your unique life.

After the devotion, you'll find a short prayer to help you take in everything that emerged from your quiet time with the Lord. Finally, your weekly devotion will end with a goal for the week—something actionable and practical for creating healthy boundaries in your life.

At the end of every quarter, you'll find a special entry called Check In with the Lord. This important element will help you take stock of the progress you have made and look forward to where you are going and where God is leading you. Each Check In with the Lord entry is formatted like a journal, with questions you can reflect on that will help you make everything stick in your mind.

One of the best things you can do for yourself right now is to commit a small block of time each week, such as Sunday evening or Monday morning, to dedicate to these weekly devotionals. Scheduling this on your calendar and protecting this time is, all by itself, an important step in creating healthy boundaries in your life.

There is a rhythm and reason to the order of the devotions—each of the weeks builds upon the previous one. This devotional is therefore not intended to be a "pick and choose" kind of book. Instead, it presents the material much the way you'd experience it if you were to come and see me for weekly sessions in pastoral counseling. For that reason, it's best to work through the devotions in the order they are presented.

Before beginning, consider how you would like to use this devotional. If you are planning on self-study, it might be a good idea to get a blank journal to use with it to write down your feelings and thoughts over the course of each week. Journaling is a great practice to help you see deeper into the patterns and thoughts that arise and are sometimes forgotten or missed.

The more committed you are to using this book the way it is intended, the better equipped you will be to create strong and lasting boundaries that lead you to the life God is calling you to!

Trust in God for Guidance

Jesus said in Mark 10:27, "All things are possible with God." You can find joy and contentment when you depend on God and are open with Him. This book is a conduit for that. Setting boundaries is a process, and it will take time to grow into this new way of setting them in your own life. Embrace the grace, love, and guidance God has for you. He led you to this resource, and because of that, there is so much hope for your future.

This journey will not always be easy. You will make mistakes, but you will also make strides. Eventually you will learn new habits that work for your life—ones that are rooted in the truth and God's love for you. Trust that He knows what you need and be open to going where He leads.

"'For I know the plans I have for you,' declares the Lord, 'plans to prosper you and not to harm you, plans to give you hope and a future'" (Jeremiah 29:11).

WEEK 1

What Is Healthy?

"But the fruit of the Spirit is love, joy, peace, forbearance, kindness, goodness, faithfulness, gentleness, and self-control. Against such things there is no law."

—GALATIANS 5:22–23

You've undoubtedly picked up this devotional to help build healthier relationships in your life. But how should health be understood by a Christian? Emotional and spiritual health can be defined by the fruit of the Spirit. In fact, Paul, the author of this passage, says that the presence of these fruits is entirely positive, without reservation or rules against them.

God wants us to live healthy and restored lives through Him that reflect the fruit of the Spirit.

God's plan is for you to experience love, joy, and peace. He wants you to be patient, kind, good, faithful, gentle, and exhibit self-control. This is God's definition of health. If we examine ourselves and realize that the fruit of the Spirit is malnourished in our lives, then we know there is an opportunity for growth through Jesus. But how?

Boundaries are an essential component of having holistic health as a Christian. Perhaps the weight of burdens and obligations is robbing you of the fullness of the fruit of the Spirit. Could you love more fully, experience greater joy, and live in deeper peace if you were able to free yourself of the guilt and pressure that comes from a lack of boundaries? Would your kindness, gentleness, and self-control grow if you had a better understanding of what you're capable of and what is healthy for you personally?

We all want to have the balanced and complete life Paul describes as the fruit of the Spirit. To do so, we need a new level of purpose and intentionality as we make choices to foster health for ourselves the way God defines it and create fertile soil for the fruit to grow.

> **Prayer:** God, I desire your health in my life. Help me evaluate myself and my decisions so I can honestly see myself and where I am right now. I want to embody your fruit more fully in my life, and I ask that you help me better understand how boundaries are important for my overall health. Amen.

> **Goal for the Week:** Daydream about the life of health and completeness God has in store for you. Examine the fruit of the Spirit in your life, particularly as it pertains to your relationships and obligations. How do you think the fruit will grow if you establish effective boundaries? How do you hope boundaries will enable you to accomplish all God has in store for you? Which of the fruits do you want more of in your life? Are there any behaviors or actions you can control that are prohibiting this fruit from ripening? What is one simple boundary you can put in place this week to step forward?

WEEK 2

Even Jesus Set Boundaries

"As they were coming down the mountain, Jesus instructed them, 'Don't tell anyone what you have seen, until the Son of Man has been raised from the dead.'"

—MATTHEW 17:9

Yes, even Jesus set some boundaries with others. In fact, there are 23 Bible verses about Jesus concealing His true identity! Jesus's ministry was purposefully orchestrated and He depended heavily on the direction of the Holy Spirit to know when to conceal or reveal information to others. This was not malicious or sneaky on His part, but rather a form of protection orchestrated by God Himself.

Jesus understood the value of His time, energy, and focus, and took steps to steward how He used His own personal resources. If Jesus had not been careful, God's entire plan for Jesus's ministry would have been thwarted.

Imagine for a moment if Jesus didn't have appropriate boundaries. He would have been constantly overwhelmed with the demands and needs of the people around Him, who sought healing, food, and other miraculous interventions. Instead, Jesus was purposeful and intentional in His use of time and energy to make the most of what He could offer. If Jesus didn't help everyone around Him, then how can we expect to help everyone ourselves?

We all need boundaries. It's not safe or wise to be everything for everyone. We are not God and we are not capable of that kind of boundless generosity. This doesn't demote our love or care for others, and astuteness is a concept Jesus Himself promoted. When we depend on the Lord for wisdom, He will guide us on what we should reveal or conceal, just as He did for Jesus.

> **Prayer:** God, help me be wise like Jesus. Help me know what boundaries to set and when to implement them. Please give me your wisdom and strength to walk this new road I am traveling. Increase in me an awareness of your direction on when to act just like Jesus. Amen.

> **Goal for the Week:** Try to envision what Jesus's experience would have been like without boundaries. How much more difficult would it have been for Him to accomplish His mission if He struggled to maintain control over His own time and energy? Now, compare how Jesus handled boundaries with the way you do. Do you think your approach to thinking about boundaries compares or contrasts with Jesus's approach? Would you like to maintain boundaries the way Jesus did? What are some simple steps you can take this week to incorporate more of Jesus's perspective on boundaries into your life?

WEEK 3

Your Foundation for Boundaries

"Therefore everyone who hears these words of mine and puts them into practice is like a wise man who built his house on the rock. But everyone who hears these words of mine and does not put them into practice is like a foolish man who built his house on sand."

—MATTHEW 7:24, 26

Jesus ended His great Sermon on the Mount by encouraging us to make Him the foundation of our life. Everything Jesus taught pointed to making Him the source of all we do. Placing Jesus at the center of our life, the center of our work, the center of our relationships, and the center of our hopes and dreams is how we build a life on the rock.

However, when we struggle to place Jesus at the center, we inevitably begin relying on our own limited strength or take on more than we can handle. When we act before we think or pray about it, we're actually building on the sand—which will eventually lead to a collapse.

Jesus's way of life is our model, and it will look different in each of us because we all are uniquely made. God isn't calling you to be a carbon copy of Jesus, but He is leading you to be yourself in Jesus.

When your decisions are based on God's leadership, you build a firmer foundation for health and wholeness in your life. God doesn't want you to be everything to everyone. Rather, Jesus wants you to take Him as the source for your decisions and depend on Him to be your guide.

God wants you to stand on solid ground, by making decisions with His guidance. When you do, you will never fall, never collapse, and you'll become unshakable in the Lord.

> **Prayer:** God, I want to stand on firmer ground. I desire you more and more, I know you are the answer to all the problems I face in this world. Help me make my decisions through you, so I am planted on a solid foundation. Amen.

> **Goal for the Week:** What does building your life on solid ground look like? How do your decisions lead you to stand on a firm foundation in the Lord? How often do you stop and think about what you do? How often do you pray before you act? These reflective questions are not meant to bring about shame or regret, but rather are an opportunity for change by looking closely at the choices you make and whether they support building a strong, solid foundation in the Lord. When you are finished reflecting, ask yourself what boundaries you need to set to help you establish a firm foundation in God.

WEEK 4

Do You Have a Plan?

"But the plans of the Lord stand firm forever, the purposes of his heart through all generations."

—PSALM 33:11

Envisioning who you want to be is a foundational element of creating boundaries. Do you want to have more peace? Do you want more time to do the things you like? Are you tired of taking on other people's problems? Do you wish your career had advanced further by this point in your life? Would you like your relationships to be better?

God made many plans in Scripture, known as covenants. From Genesis to Jesus, God had a plan to bring a Redeemer into the world to save us. In this way, God shows us that planning is good, wise, and helps us achieve the life He is calling all of us to—one of peace, joy, and love.

You undoubtedly have many questions about your own future and life plans, and these inquiries will help shape the path you follow in the future. One of the best ways to ensure that your plans stay on track is through the healthy use of boundaries. You need guiding principles to stay grounded and navigate the various challenges that will arrive on your journey. Boundaries are important decisions you can make now that provide a supportive framework when unexpected circumstances arise and you need to make solid decisions under stress and time pressure.

All change requires a plan. When you know where you want to go, who you want to be, and how you want to feel inside, then you will be able to create a map to take you there. For example, to improve fitness and health, a person must follow a diet and exercise plan that will get them the results they want. The same principle applies to relationships and who you want to be in them. You will succeed if you know where you want to go and then create a plan to get there.

> **Prayer:** God, help me craft a plan for my life that will lead me closer to you and your likeness. Thank you for staying true to your plan and bringing redemption through Christ. Open up possibilities in my life that come from planning in and through you. Amen.

> **Goal for the Week:** Take time to dream about your life over the next 3, 6, and 12 months. Who do you want to become? What do you want your emotional health to look like? What do you want your relationships to be like? How about your career or family? Write down some of your biggest desires and craft a plan for how you will get there. Consider whether you are taking on too much or whether this plan is reasonable for your life. How will you create boundaries to help you follow through with this plan?

WEEK 5

How to Say No

"For the Spirit God gave us does not make us timid, but gives us power, love, and self-discipline."

—2 TIMOTHY 1:7

If you have trouble saying no, then this is your power verse! So many of us have issues with saying no, usually because we feel obligated or simply don't want to be uncomfortable. Our motivations can also be misdirected, leading us to think we should be doing more because "God wants me to." There is often a lot of baggage that surrounds the ability to say no. But it is the foundation of setting good boundaries.

Saying no needs to be purposeful and clear, with reason and intention. Could saying no provide more space in your life, ease your burdens, and enable you to work where you truly feel called? Imagine a person who feels led by God to serve in missions at church, but they are instead asked to help with the children's Sunday school. They say yes to Sunday school because they fear they will let someone down if they don't. However, they are not likely to feel fulfilled in Sunday school, because it is not where God was leading them. They start to regret their decision, want to skip church, and are deflated about the whole situation.

Being able to say no can be a positive action when it's based on the truth that you simply cannot always do everything that could potentially be asked of you or always be who others expect you to be. Although saying no may never feel fully comfortable in the moment, you will learn over time the value that comes from being honest about what's possible at any given moment and what aligns with your own needs.

A person who has boundaries will be able to confidently and lovingly say no to offers that don't fit their plan. They do not get themselves into situations where they will not thrive. This is the power of saying no wisely. Trust in God's purpose for you, and prayerfully evaluate when you need to say no.

> **Prayer:** God, help me boldly and lovingly say no to more things in my life. Help me draw on your strength, power, and self-control when I say no. Lord, please help me feel more comfortable and free to lovingly say no to things that don't fit into the plan you and I have created. Amen.

> **Goal for the Week:** Spend time journaling about the feelings you experience from saying no. Does saying no make you feel uncomfortable, scared, selfish? Do you sometimes struggle to say no just to avoid these feelings? Next, envision scenarios where you lovingly say no to things that don't fit into your plan. What feelings arise when you think about lovingly saying no? God is calling you to be motivated by Him, not by what others will think. How can you create a boundary to help your "no" be more purposeful and in line with God's plan for you?

WEEK 6

When to Say Yes

"All you need to say is simply 'Yes' or 'No'; anything beyond this comes from the evil one."

—MATTHEW 5:37

Can you imagine if Jesus said yes to everyone? Would Jesus have been able to accomplish all He did if He was constantly busy with tasks that were out of the scope of God's plan and will? Jesus was on a mission. He knew where He was going and what He had to do to get there. Modeling Jesus in this way is your secret weapon for knowing when to say yes.

It can be hard to say yes to the things that will support the person you want to be, especially if you are someone who says yes a lot. You must be wise about when to say yes in a way that will reinforce your goals and your boundaries. Having a plan for when to say yes will make this decision easier.

Understanding your own personal boundaries and adhering to them will enable you to say yes to the things that you really want, rather than simply agreeing to anything asked of you. You will quickly find that you're more grounded and satisfied with your choices when you take more control over what you say yes to.

One of the hardest issues Christians have about saying yes wisely is the reality that there will often be many offers that come along that seem like the things God wants us to do. That's why you need to create a blueprint for yourself to help you process the offers that should lead you to say yes. Ask yourself questions such as, "Do I have time for this, or will I need to make more time?" When you are able to discern what things in life are important and what are distractions, then your yes becomes very powerful and purposeful. And in this way, you will be navigating choices and decisions in the same way that Jesus did.

> **Prayer:** God, please develop in me the wisdom that Jesus had as He walked this earth. Help me see when I should purposefully say yes so that I go where you are leading me. I thank you for the ability to lean on you as I learn how to intentionally say yes. Amen.

> **Goal for the Week:** Create a personal blueprint for how to decide when to say yes. Begin by writing down your big goals and desires, and where you believe God is leading you. Then create a list of the most important questions to ask yourself before saying yes to a commitment. Your questions might include: Do I have the time to do this well? Am I excited about this idea? Does this align with where I believe God is leading me? What will I miss if I say no? Create a document with your questions, and spend time reviewing and internalizing it so that these questions become second nature—which is, in itself, an important boundary.

WEEK 7

How Much Time Are You Giving to Yourself?

"The apostles gathered around Jesus and reported to him all they had done and taught. Then, because so many people were coming and going that they did not even have a chance to eat, he said to them, 'Come with me by yourselves to a quiet place and get some rest.'"

—MARK 6:30–31

Jesus was well known for performing miracles and giving powerful sermons. But what did He do after those accomplishments? He usually retreated to privacy! Jesus's ministry in this world was only three years, and He spent that time wisely and purposefully. He didn't use every second He had to serve or perform miracles. Rather, He depended on the Father to help Him know when to act, and Jesus drew His strength from His quiet time with God.

Jesus took breaks!

If we are following in the footsteps of Jesus, we too are called to take breaks to refuel and refresh our energy. Our bodies and minds are designed for periodic intentional rest. But we often struggle to stop for a break, or to take the time to enjoy the things we like.

Sometimes feelings of guilt surround taking a break, leading us to think that rest means we are being selfish or even un-Christlike. But that's not the reality. If God intended us to serve and give of ourselves 24/7, then we wouldn't have a need for Him. Instead, we would be more robot than human being—but even robots need a battery recharge!

It can feel noble and right to be always giving of yourself, but that will only lead to bitterness and burnout. Rest is such an important concept that God made it one of the Ten Commandments, to help stop the tendency we humans have to do too much! If God actually commanded that we take a whole day to rest every week, this shows us the importance of periodically resting and recharging in Him.

> **Prayer:** God, thank you for the call to rest in you. Thank you for taking my burdens and helping me to rest. Help me take some purposeful and restful time for myself, because I need it so much. Show me the rhythms of how you want me to spend my time. Amen.

> **Goal for the Week:** Review your rest and relaxation time over the course of a week. How much time do you take for yourself? (Hint: Doing this devotion is taking good quality time for yourself.) Add up all the time you take for yourself and evaluate what it tells you. Do you need more time for yourself, or do you need to find better ways to use your time to find purposeful rest and relaxation? Create a boundary that will protect your desire to take some "me time" each week and make a plan to implement it in your life.

WEEK 8

Relationships Are Hard

"Now Cain said to his brother Abel, 'Let's go out to the field.' While they were in the field, Cain attacked his brother Abel and killed him."

—GENESIS 4:8

Only four chapters into the Bible, and the first children of Adam and Eve were so troubled that one killed the other. Relationships have been hard for humans from the beginning! In fact, relationship problems are a common theme in Scripture, from Cain and Abel to Joseph and his brothers, to James and Jesus, and Paul and Peter. Relationship problems are real and affect everyone.

The challenges you experience in your relationships are no different than those in the Bible. I hope knowing you are not alone in this brings you some comfort.

In fact, I have never encountered a single person in my ministry who hasn't had at least one major relationship problem in their lives. It's important to understand that relationships are always hard, because knowing that provides perspective and helps us feel less isolated.

Understanding that relationships are inherently hard is part of the process of creating boundaries in your life. If you readily accept this concept instead of fighting it, you'll be able to find peace in knowing the truth about the nature of relationships. Healthy relationships have good boundaries that enable them to flourish and thrive. Without boundaries, relationships tend to become overreaching, burdensome, and typically lead to chaos.

This is part of life, but it doesn't have to determine our path. Because we have Jesus, we also have the ability to grow in His likeness and to take on His way of life. Since God is always with us, we have the tools necessary to build healthy relationships—even from the hard ones.

> **Prayer:** God, I need your help for guidance and strength in my relationships. I want healthy bonds with others, and I need your wisdom on how to set the right boundaries in my life. Please lead me to healthy and strong relationships through creating the right and proper boundaries. Amen.

> **Goal for the Week:** Spend time this week contemplating your relationships, past and present. Identify three easy relationships in your life, ones that have been stress-free, with minimal conflict, and generally work well. What makes these relationships easy? Are they close connections or casual acquaintances? Next, identify three difficult relationships. Why are these relationships more challenging? How do the difficult relationships compare with the easier ones? Are there any commonalities between both kinds of relationships? Do your best to identify the characteristics that make each easy or difficult. Assess what this information is telling you and how you can set boundaries that reinforce the types of relationships you are seeking.

WEEK 9

Do You Have Clear Expectations?

"Two blind men were sitting by the roadside, and when they heard that Jesus was going by, they shouted, 'Lord, Son of David, have mercy on us!' The crowd rebuked them and told them to be quiet, but they shouted all the louder, 'Lord, Son of David, have mercy on us!' Jesus stopped and called them. 'What do you want me to do for you?' he asked. 'Lord,' they answered, 'we want our sight.'"

—MATTHEW 20:30–33

Do you actively ask others, "What is expected of me" when you are asked to help? As we see in this passage, Jesus asked that very question! Of course, Jesus almost certainly understood what the two blind men were seeking, but He still had the wisdom to make them specifically state what they wanted. There was no ambiguity in the interaction between Jesus and these two men because Jesus was up-front and transparent about the communication. Perhaps Jesus was demonstrating an important model for all of us in this scene.

When others ask for our help, we should be very clear in our communications and expectations. Many conflicts and misunderstandings occur when two parties are not clear about their initial expectations of each other. Have you ever found yourself in a situation where each side thought they were signing up for something completely different?

Clear expectations are critical for good boundaries, because expectations function as a type of contract where each side makes an agreement about what will be done. This will eliminate many problems up front and provide a foundation for processing issues that do arise in the future. Expectations don't need to be stiff or formal, just clear and practical.

You can model Jesus's actions by always making the effort to intentionally understand what others want or expect from you. In this way, you can protect both sides from hurt and misunderstanding that could have easily been prevented at the beginning.

> **Prayer:** Lord, I come to you asking for the ability to be lovingly bold in expressing clear communication when others need something from me. Help me walk in line with Jesus, who modeled a way to help that is clear and practical. Help me be bold and vigilant in understanding the expectations of others. Amen.

> **Goal for the Week:** Recall a time when you discovered hidden expectations after agreeing to offer your help or service. What was that like for you? Try to remember the emotions you experienced. Would it have been better if you had clearly stated what you were capable and not capable of doing? How might your past experience(s) inform your future? What boundary can you create that will help you avoid hidden expectations?

WEEK 10

Prayer Is a Way to Help

"Then Jesus told his disciples a parable to show them that they should always pray and not give up."

—LUKE 18:1

Without boundaries, our love and compassion can lead us into circumstances where we desperately want to help someone who frankly doesn't want our assistance at the moment. Our heart might be moved to rescue a person struggling with dangerous behavior, addiction, or unfortunate circumstances, but we also need to recognize we are not the savior. Jesus is.

When Jesus returned to Nazareth, He came with the same teachings and miracles that had been witnessed by many others throughout the region. But the people in His own hometown couldn't bring themselves to accept Jesus as the Son of God. They questioned Him, instead of simply accepting what He had to offer. Jesus was clearly disappointed by their response, but He moved on with the mission of God and didn't give up.

If someone doesn't want direct help, there is always an opportunity to channel love and compassion in a different way. Begin by approaching the Lord in prayer, asking Him to bring about healing and change. Seek His wisdom in understanding the best way to love and care for those you are concerned about.

Some situations in life are completely beyond our control, but we always have the powerful possibilities of prayer. If you value prayer and what it can do, then it will help you establish an important boundary—the one that means you will not worry and burden yourself with attempting to help those who don't want it. Even if someone doesn't want your help, you can do immeasurable good by always praying for them.

> **Prayer:** Lord, help me increase my prayer life. For those I am worried about, please help me cling to you through prayer. I know you are good and hear the concerns of my heart. Help me release the burdens of people I love and worry about and entrust them to you through prayer. Amen.

> **Goal for the Week:** Consider a person in your life who has you worried about the choices they are making. Evaluate the emotions you have tied up in the situation. Try to write down every feeling you have about it. Is this situation weighing you down? Is it affecting your health? How can you bring your relationship with God into it? How can prayer be an asset for you in this difficult situation? Create a boundary that will help you latch on to God and prayer as a way to bring peace and health to your heart.

WEEK 11

Are You a People Pleaser?

"Am I now trying to win the approval of human beings, or of God? Or am I trying to please people? If I were still trying to please people, I would not be a servant of Christ."

—GALATIANS 1:10

While serving as a minister in a church, I once worked closely with a man who struggled with a constant desire to please other people. To him, keeping others happy and pleased felt like the Christian way to behave. I shared with him a completely different perspective on the matter, based on my understanding of Scripture. One of the important verses on this topic is this week's Scripture passage.

But even beyond Paul's words in Galatians, the entire scope of Scripture directly reinforces the reality that we are not called to please people, but instead to follow God's call and direction in our lives. Unfortunately, human beings are often fickle and unstable. People change their minds and frequently have hidden motives and pressures that they may not even be aware of. Trying to please people means having to stand on the shifting sands of their desires. However, seeking to please God means taking root in solid ground, because God is always stable and has no secret agendas or motives.

God is the only thing that can truly fill us up and restore us. People pleasing will never be a satisfying solution to life's problems, because it means trying to fill a deficit in others that can never be truly filled. We can't depend on people and their approval to be our source of security. That's why pleasing God first should be our primary motivation. We can trust that God's way is good and will produce the life we desire.

> **Prayer:** God, please help me have you as the focus and motivation for all that I do. I know living in this stance will help more people and give me more peace. Let me cling to you and your way as my compass, instead of clinging to a fear of how others will receive me. Amen.

> **Goal for the Week:** Evaluate your motivations for the things you do. Do you find yourself motivated by how others will respond? If so, is your emotional well-being tied up with this? For instance, if others do not receive your actions positively, does this hurt you or even depress you? And on the flip side, do you feel relief or even bliss if others warmly receive your actions? Now, imagine working for God's approval instead of the approval of others. How does that make you feel and what thoughts does it raise? If this resonates with you, focus on what boundary you can create that will help you be motivated by God instead of others.

WEEK 12

Who Do You Need to Forgive?

"Then Peter came to Jesus and asked, 'Lord, how many times shall I forgive my brother or sister who sins against me? Up to seven times?' Jesus answered, 'I tell you, not seven times, but seventy-seven times.'"

—MATTHEW 18:21–22

Forgiveness is an intriguing concept because it has the capacity to set one free, but it's widely misunderstood. Sometimes forgiveness is viewed as weakness or capitulating to injustice. Make no mistake, forgiveness is hard. It goes against our natural defense mechanisms for self-protection.

But when God calls us to forgive, He doesn't necessarily mean we have to restore the relationship. Yes, reconciliation can happen, but more importantly, forgiveness is for our inner being, because a lack of forgiveness is a powerful chamber that can imprison us and cultivate bitterness, anger, and broken emotions. Jesus wants all of us to be whole and healthy in and through Him. Forgiveness isn't about how we feel, but rather a choice to move forward. It's an opportunity to heal.

For instance, my dad wasn't a safe man, and I had no contact with him for the last 20 years of his life. When I decided to forgive him, it was between God and me. My dad actually never knew I forgave him, because it wasn't about him—it was about God, myself, and what God wanted to heal in me. Over the course of 20 years, I have had to forgive my father multiple times, as new memories and issues from the past arise.

Every time I choose forgiveness over bitterness and hurt, I grow with God. God makes it possible for me to forgive, and this enables me to grow more in His image. Learning that forgiveness is more about your health and completeness in Christ is a vital piece to your happiness.

> **Prayer:** God, lead me through the process of forgiveness where it is needed. Let me rest in you to gain my strength and the direction to forgive those who have hurt me. Enable me to have peace and patience as I journey with you to forgive like Jesus. Amen.

> **Goal for the Week:** Has there been someone in your life who has caused you pain that you haven't forgiven? Over this next week, bring the pain you have experienced to God and express your hesitation to forgive. Make this your prayer practice this week, speaking to God as much as you can about a person you haven't forgiven. God already knows it is difficult for you to forgive, and He will lead you through the process of slowly learning what forgiveness looks like for you in this circumstance.

WEEK 13

Finding Your Voice

"Jesus answered, 'Even if I testify on my own behalf, my testimony is valid, for I know where I came from and where I am going. But you have no idea where I come from or where I am going. You judge by human standards; I pass judgment on no one. But if I do judge, my decisions are true, because I am not alone. I stand with the Father, who sent me. In your own Law it is written that the testimony of two witnesses is true. I am one who testifies for myself; my other witness is the Father, who sent me.'"

—**JOHN 8:14–18**

Have you ever wished you had spoken up and expressed your opinion, but didn't? Perhaps you were afraid or too timid to speak up. If so, please know that many of us struggle with this issue! Learning how to appropriately use your voice is an integral component of creating good boundaries in your life.

It can sometimes be difficult to express your thoughts and feelings about a situation because of the fear of how others will interpret them. Many people simply do not like to share what they feel because they are scared of the consequences of expressing themselves. But when you are unable to express your thoughts in a healthy way, it often leads to feeling misunderstood, unimportant, dismissed, and, ultimately, angry.

God made each of us unique, and every one of us has their own perspective. As long as you express yourself with loving honesty, you should not fear the consequences of what people may think or say. Learning to speak truth in love is the way of a disciple—someone who is walking in Jesus's footsteps of grace and love.

Our words, spoken through God's lead, have the power to heal, restore, and bring hope. We can be agents of God's love and truth in the world. But sometimes we are too afraid to speak. Just remember, your words have power and can be used as a catalyst for good, for yourself and others. As you grow in your understanding of boundaries, you will also find your own voice develop within you.

> **Prayer:** Lord, help me find my voice in you. Guide me to speak when I feel I need to say something in truth and love. Help me conquer the fear of what others might think or do. I do not want to shrink away, but I want to be bold in your grace and truth. Amen.

> **Goal for the Week:** Spend time this week journaling on the following questions. Do you ever hold back what you think or feel because you're afraid of what others will think or say? When you do express your opinion, does it come from a foundation of God's love and truth, or something much different? Do you ever regret what you've said or regret not saying anything at all? What does all of this tell you? What is a boundary that can help you better express yourself in loving ways?

Check In with the Lord

Envision who you want to be a year from now. What types of relationships do you want to have? How do you want to feel inside, day to day? More peaceful, more stable, less fearful, a stronger sense of worth?

Now take all of those goals and hopes for the coming year and bring them before the Lord. Spend time with God, write down your prayers and concerns, and ask Him to help you see the potential for your life that will come from healthy boundaries. Thank God for this journey you are following.

_____
_____
_____
_____
_____
_____
_____
_____
_____
_____
_____
_____

WEEK 14

Time Management

"Be very careful, then, how you live—not as unwise but as wise, making the most of every opportunity, because the days are evil. Therefore do not be foolish, but understand what the Lord's will is."

—EPHESIANS 5:15–17

Have you ever thought about how some people seem to accomplish so much in their limited amount of time? Have you ever wondered how others have so much time to rest and enjoy life? We all have the same 24 hours in a day but how we use the time, and the boundaries we create to guard our time, make all the difference.

It may often feel like time is out of our control, but the decisions we make moment to moment dictate how each of us spends our day. Many of the decisions we make each day about how to use our time are set on autopilot as we follow the familiar patterns of life. For example, you might travel several minutes out of your way to pick up breakfast from the same bakery each morning, never realizing the time you could save each week by having breakfast at home. Or perhaps you always feel pressed against deadlines at work and don't take into account all the time you spend browsing social media on your phone. So if you struggle with getting the most out of a day, start by checking the choices you make on autopilot.

Of course, we all have responsibilities; I know this very well as a mother of two little kids with special needs. But even with all of the needs of my children, I still have complete control of how I use my time. I map out the essentials of each day, such as work, self-care, childcare, and exercise, and constantly search for how to fit in space for myself and my personal hobbies and interests, to keep me healthy and balanced.

Learning how to take responsibility for the way we use our time and knowing how to make more conscious choices about how we spend it is a valuable tool for cultivating a more fulfilling and purposeful life. Paul reminds us in Ephesians that our time, and each opportunity, has great value.

> **Prayer:** Lord, you know how much is on my plate each day, and you also know my hopes and my dreams. Help me clearly see how I use my time. Lead me to be aware of where I am wasting time and where I need to find more time for taking care of myself—and having fun. Amen.

> **Goal for the Week:** Evaluate how you use your time. How much of your time is productive? How much is spent in relaxation or downtime? How many time-wasters do you have in your life? Look over your week and create a pie chart or graph of how you currently use your time. When you are finished, ask yourself if you are happy with your use of time. Would you like your graph to look different? If so, what do you need to do to change how you use your time? What things do you need to say no to so you can have more time for what you really want to do?

WEEK 15

Don't Let Others Steal Your Confidence in God

"Sometimes you were publicly exposed to insult and persecution; at other times you stood side by side with those who were so treated. You suffered along with those in prison and joyfully accepted the confiscation of your property, because you knew that you yourselves had better and lasting possessions. So do not throw away your confidence; it will be richly rewarded. You need to persevere so that when you have done the will of God, you will receive what he has promised."

—HEBREWS 10:33–36

Have you ever felt moved by God to share or do something in His name, only to be met with a lackluster response, or even ridicule? Many Christians have experienced this while stepping out in faith—myself included. This is, unfortunately, a common experience for anyone serving God.

But you can create personal boundaries that will enable you to remain positive and confident in your service, even if it isn't well received. What is most important is how God sees your work—even more so than those you help—and boundaries can help you remain in that truth.

Many faithful Christian leaders have abandoned service and doing good in God's truth because of the hurtful words and actions others have directed at them. But remember, if people are the source of your stability, you will eventually succumb to their fickleness. This quote from Hebrews is telling us that God is aware of all we do, even if no one else notices or cares. Don't allow yourself to lose confidence in God's call on your life because of what other people might say to you.

The Lord sees everything we do, and this week's Scripture tells us that doing the will of God will bring about rewards despite what others may say or do. We can't control how other people act. That's why we need boundaries to help us guard against criticism and remind us that we are working for God first and foremost. We have the choice to remain confident in God, whatever circumstances we face.

> **Prayer:** Lord, please help me have my confidence in you at all times, even if others do not receive it well. Create in me eyes to see your call on my life and spur me on to follow where you call me. I want to be confident through only you. Amen.

> **Goal for the Week:** Do you often make decisions about your words and actions based on how well they will be received? How often do you reflect on what God thinks about what you're doing or how you are serving as He wants you to? How can boundaries help you guard against being motivated by others' approval rather than God's calling?

WEEK 16

When to Walk Away

"When Jesus heard that John had been put in prison, he withdrew to Galilee."

—MATTHEW 4:12

Did you know that Jesus sometimes walked away from others? In fact, much of Jesus's ministry was purposefully in the countryside, to protect His mission and His life. Jesus knew that if He stuck around the Temple and the concentrated oppression found in Jerusalem, His life would be in danger. He didn't return to Jerusalem until God's plan for the cross and the empty grave was ready. Until then, Jesus concealed His identity and ministered primarily outside of Jerusalem.

Understanding how Jesus did and didn't show himself publicly is crucial for Christians, because it teaches us that there is an appropriate time to withdraw. Jesus didn't hide because He was scared. Rather, He walked away because it was the wise thing to do and it was in line with the will and plan of God.

We too are sometimes called to walk away from a situation or a relationship. We may think God would certainly want us to stay to extend more love or to fix whatever is wrong. But these thoughts will lead us to endlessly work on things that are too big for us to fix alone. The world is filled with people hurting, wrongs that need righting, and work that needs doing. But even

Jesus didn't do everything possible while He was on this earth. To carry out God's plan, sometimes Jesus walked away.

In this week's Scripture, Jesus walked away because he was in real physical danger. We may not always be at risk of physical harm, but we need to value ourselves and establish boundaries that allow us to leave when any kind of harm is possible. We must be wise and not allow ourselves to be put in situations that are dangerous to our mind, body, and faith. That is why we must sometimes walk away.

> **Prayer:** God, please develop in me your wisdom and discernment to know when to walk away, as Jesus did. Sometimes I can get confused about what to do, but I want to trust in your direction, and I need to hear your call more loudly. Amen.

> **Goal for the Week:** Imagine Jesus's ministry, including the level of threat and danger He faced at every turn. Now envision all the suffering Jesus saw in the brokenness around Him. Do you think it was hard for Him to walk away from all the people in Jerusalem in order to save His own life? Do you think He did the right thing? How can this understanding of Jesus help you find the right steps to take in your own life? What boundaries might you create that are in line with Jesus walking away from danger?

WEEK 17

You Are Worthy

"For you created my inmost being; you knit me together in my mother's womb. I praise you because I am fearfully and wonderfully made; your works are wonderful, I know that full well."

—PSALM 139:13–14

When God created you, He did so with purpose, love, and intentionality. God knows you intimately and sees immense value in you, no matter what you do. But you might fall into the trap of defining your self-worth by your successes and failures, not your inherent value to God. While we all make mistakes and are not perfect, your failures and flaws do not define your worth.

Healthy boundaries are difficult to create when you don't see your own worth. There is nothing that can separate you from God's love, and even your shortcomings (real or perceived) will not stop God from seeing your profound value and that you are worthy of His love, guidance, and protection.

A big step in creating healthy boundaries is to accept your shortcomings and receive God's immeasurable love. You don't need to earn value in God's eyes. You're already worthy because God created you. You are His child, and your value to Him is priceless.

On my personal journey of creating healthy boundaries, I was best equipped when I wrapped myself in God's love instead of focusing on everything I thought was wrong with me. It was then that I was able to see my true value—which is given by God and cannot be changed or altered by any human being.

God's love will build you up and bring healing. It's a necessary piece in all relationships because God is the source of all love. His love helps you create meaningful and lasting healthy boundaries as He boosts your self-worth and leads you to look beyond your flaws.

> **Prayer:** God, please speak into the places of my heart that are feeling low and lacking value. Restore in me awareness of your goodness and affection. Help me cling to your love as I walk with you on this new path of boundaries in my life. Amen.

> **Goal for the Week:** Healthy boundaries cannot be created and maintained without a strong sense of self-worth and love. Your goal this week is to evaluate and work on your self-worth. On a scale of 1 to 10, how highly do you value yourself? As you evaluate your current place on the scale, reflect on the Scripture for this week. How does it inform your sense of worth and self-love? Does the Scripture and devotion help you step more into God's love for you? If so, how and why? What boundary can you create this week that is rooted in self-value and God's love?

WEEK 18

Are You Out of Balance?

"As Jesus and his disciples were on their way, he came to a village where a woman named Martha opened her home to him. She had a sister called Mary, who sat at the Lord's feet listening to what he said. But Martha was distracted by all the preparations that had to be made. She came to him and asked, 'Lord, don't you care that my sister has left me to do the work by myself? Tell her to help me!' 'Martha, Martha,' the Lord answered, 'you are worried and upset about many things, but few things are needed—or indeed only one. Mary has chosen what is better, and it will not be taken away from her.'"

—LUKE 10:38–42

Most people will tell you that it's better to be working, serving, and helping others. But in this story of Martha and Mary, we see that Jesus was more impressed with Mary. While Martha was the great hostess of the dinner party, it was Mary who sat at the feet of Jesus, doing nothing to help—which was very unusual for that period of time. The tradition then was that the women served the men and made sure all the guest of honor's needs were met. Instead, Mary broke with custom and simply wanted to be near Jesus and listen to His words.

This story in Scripture illuminates the importance of balance. While we all are called to serve, we also are led to rest and recharge in the Lord. Both are vital for our completeness in Christ, and for our peace and happiness. And we need to set boundaries that help us achieve this goal. Our service should always be done out of love for Christ. If that is why we are serving, then we also need to refuel and recharge in the Lord regularly, because He is our source of strength.

Christ wants us to have a balance in our lives between rest and service. God knows balance is for our own good. There's nothing wrong with being Martha and working hard and well. But don't forget that we all need to be Mary sometimes too, and simply sit with Jesus.

> **Prayer:** Lord, please open my eyes to see where my life is out of balance. I need your guidance to explore ways I can find health and balance in my daily life. Thank you for caring so much for me that you desire me to be whole in you. Amen.

> **Goal for the Week:** Reread this week's passage from Luke. Do you identify more with Mary or Martha? In what ways are you similar to and different from each of these women? What would a blend of Mary and Martha's actions look like in your life? What do you imagine a balanced approach to service and rest would look like? What kind of boundaries are necessary in your life to have a more balanced approach to work and rest? What is a step you can take this week to foster more balance in your life?

WEEK 19

Are You Too Available?

"There is a time for everything, and a season for every activity under the heavens: a time to be born and a time to die, a time to plant and a time to uproot."

—ECCLESIASTES 3:1–2

In our modern world, most of us have multiple ways for people to reach us through social media, email, and our phones. It seems like we're always available. But being available 24/7 isn't really healthy; it can lead to anxiety, exhaustion, and imbalance.

Just because you can be reached at any time doesn't mean you should always be available. For example, issues at work can often take advantage of that instant accessibility, leading you to be consumed with obligations when you should be resting. Other times, we're the source of the problem ourselves because we are spending countless hours on our phones while neglecting what is happening around us.

Technology is a great thing, but if you don't put in place some boundaries on its use, it can rule your life. When you feel that every text, social media post, email, and news notification needs to be looked at the moment it comes through, that's a problem. Your phone may be ruling your life.

A lack of boundaries around your availability can create strains on close relationships. If you are always responding immediately to everyone who contacts you, then others around you might feel neglected or less important than whatever is happening on your phone. Placing boundaries around your accessibility creates more space for others.

And don't forget, God is always with you. Creating boundaries for your availability will also create more space in your life for your relationship with God.

Prayer: God, thank you for helping me place limitations on myself, because being available too much is not good for me. I need to rest from demands and obligations, so please help me rest in your love and grace. You are the only being who should be accessed 24/7, and I am thankful you are always available for me. Amen.

Goal for the Week: Do you have any current boundaries on your accessibility? For instance, do you always feel compelled to respond if work or other obligations arise during your downtime? Do you feel uncomfortable not dealing with communication immediately? Or do you feel the opposite and procrastinate about responding? Do any of your relationships feel stressed because of your accessibility? Consider your use of social media, emails, texts, and other forms of accessibility. When a notification comes in, do you stop everything to attend to it? Take all of the answers here and use them to create a boundary to help you have healthier accessibility (and inaccessibility) in your life.

WEEK 20

Break Through the Excuses

"When Jesus saw him lying there and learned that he had been in this condition for a long time, he asked him, 'Do you want to get well?' 'Sir,' the invalid replied, 'I have no one to help me into the pool when the water is stirred. While I am trying to get in, someone else goes down ahead of me.' Then Jesus said to him, 'Get up! Pick up your mat and walk.' At once the man was cured; he picked up his mat and walked. The day on which this took place was a Sabbath."

—JOHN 5:6–9

Jesus had a famous encounter with a man who had a legitimate excuse: He physically couldn't get to the healing pool. True to form, Jesus wasn't concerned about this man's perceived issues, and instead went straight to the root of the problem. Addressing it head on, Jesus asked the man if he wanted to get well. But the man didn't seem to know how to answer, instead offering Jesus only an excuse. Jesus ignored his excuse and simply said, "Well, get up and walk!" and at once the man was healed—through the power of Jesus's miracle, not because Jesus helped him overcome the excuse.

The key to this story is how this struggling man needed to believe and trust in Jesus and follow His call to action in order to break through the excuses. Jesus showed him that excuses were not required, and all he really needed was the presence of Christ.

It's important to limit the impact excuses have on your life. Sometimes you have no real options, and sometimes the excuse is the only real explanation. But far too often, easy excuses prevent us from having a happier and healthier life filled with peace and joy. In every life, it can sometimes feel as if there are too many barriers, and defaulting to excuses becomes an easy alternative. But that only leads us away from becoming all that Christ has called us to be in His presence and power.

> **Prayer:** Lord, despite my excuses you still move mountains and bring about healing, and for this I thank you. I do not want to be trapped in patterns of excuses, but rather I want to seek out truth and grace as I work on becoming more whole and complete in you. Help me in these desires. Amen.

> **Goal for the Week:** Examine how you use excuses and lovingly hold yourself accountable for the excuses you make. Do you find that you use excuses a lot or a little? Are the excuses you use based on real explanations for your problems? Are your excuses holding you back? Are they stopping you from pushing forward? Assess and evaluate with the Lord, asking Him to provide clarity and insight into your behavior patterns. What kind of personal boundaries can you set that will limit how you use excuses?

WEEK 21

Hidden Motivators

"I do not understand what I do. For what I want to do I do not do, but what I hate I do."

—ROMANS 7:15

Can you believe that even Paul, the great missionary of the early Christian Church, sometimes felt conflicted in understanding his motivations? This fact should give each of us peace in realizing that our personal motivations are often difficult to understand and navigate.

Every decision we make, every action we take has a motivation behind it. For example, the main reason people work is to have an income to afford to provide food, shelter, and necessities for themselves and those they love. We may not wake up daily and dress for work thinking, "If I stop going to work, I'll eventually get kicked out of my home!" But that motivation is still behind the action. The better we understand our motivations, the greater our ability to understand ourselves.

Paul openly admitted that he struggled with hidden motivations that led him to sometimes make bad decisions or wrong actions—and we would be wise to admit the same to ourselves. If we are able to recognize our true motivations, we will be better able to navigate challenging situations and understand what we truly need. For example, we may be triggered or upset by people or circumstances that remind us of past hurts. We may sometimes be aware of how we're reacting, while other times it may just feel like an automatic, subconscious response.

An important boundary you can set for yourself is not to always accept what's on the surface, but be ready and willing to challenge your hidden motivations—even if you don't do it publicly, as Paul did. When you find yourself overwhelmed by an action you've taken or a decision you must make, make it a practice to sit down with God and honestly ask what's motivating you, and whether that motivation is leading you in the right direction.

> **Prayer:** God, I desire to be complete and whole in you. Help me see and address the hidden motivators in my life that are keeping me from being who I want to be. Allow me to receive your grace and love, as I know you love me just as I am. Amen.

> **Goal for the Week:** Identify a challenging or difficult situation that's currently in your life. What are the motivations behind how you respond to these circumstances? For example, is fear, jealousy, anger, or any other negative emotion the true motivating factor? How can you establish a boundary with yourself to never allow motivations to go unexamined? What would such a boundary mean for your life personally, and how could it help you better address issues as they arise?

WEEK 22

Have a Different Perspective

"So we fix our eyes not on what is seen, but on what is unseen, since what is seen is temporary, but what is unseen is eternal."

—2 CORINTHIANS 4:18

Sometimes we can get narrow-sighted, only seeing the picture of our life from one angle. If we are able to shift our perspective a little bit, the picture becomes bigger and our understanding is challenged and expanded. Photography is a great example of this: Zoom in and we see only a small area; zoom out and we see the bigger picture.

We need to remember that our Lord sees and knows everything. But we, in our position of limited perspective, can only see and understand a little. That's why our faith in God is so important. We need Him to help broaden our perspective and guide us to see more of the big picture.

We can't see how everything will play out, but God knows what will happen and when it will happen. Recognizing that God is overseeing it all will help you rest in His providence, even when things are confusing or you are worried about how they will play out. God will lead you to a deeper understanding and a better perspective if you simply fix your eyes on Him.

Make it a habit to recognize that you don't know or see everything, but God does and you can turn to Him for help. Set that boundary with yourself.

> **Prayer:** God, you know everything and can see how everything will play out. Please help me ground myself in your knowledge and providence over every situation, problem, and fear that I have. Please expand my understanding when my perspective is limited or narrow. Amen.

> **Goal for the Week:** Take some of the burdens in your heart and play them out using the zoom lens of your mind. What does it look like to be really zoomed in to each situation? What do you see when you are very close to it? Now zoom out in your mind and allow yourself a different perspective. Invite God into this exercise and ask Him to help shape your perspective. Resolve to fix your eyes on Him rather than your own limited perspective and understanding.

WEEK 23

You Aren't Supposed to Carry It All

"So do not fear, for I am with you; do not be dismayed, for I am your God. I will strengthen you and help you; I will uphold you with my righteous right hand."

—ISAIAH 41:10

Every disciple needs to establish a firm boundary with themselves that directs them to always turn to God first for help. Yes, we are capable of accomplishing an incredible number of things, but we were never designed to do the work on our own.

As a follower of Jesus, you are able to draw on God's inner strength at any time for anything. Since the Holy Spirit lives within each believer, you have access to God at all times. And if Jesus's ministry shows us anything, it's that we can see how the world can change when we work through God's strength.

Working in our own strength can deplete our energy and even lead us to feelings of depression, anxiety, and exhaustion. But the Scripture for this week points us to the supportive nature of God. He never wants us to carry loads that we are not equipped to handle. He is our good Father and wants to tend to each of our hearts and the matters that weigh us down.

Building boundaries in your life that lead you to working in God's strength, and not just your own, will bring profound peace. Create a boundary that reminds you that you're not all on your own, and that you'll turn to Him when you feel that way. Walking in God's strength means mirroring how Jesus lived in this world. This is how Jesus was able to accomplish all that He did, and this support is available to us all.

> **Prayer:** God, I want to work through your strength and not rely on my own limited strength when yours is limitless. Please illuminate for me how to find ways to work in your strength. Please continue to be gracious with me as I work on this new boundary in my life. Amen.

> **Goal for the Week:** Stress, worry, exhaustion are usually indicators of being overburdened. Is this you? Are you a person who feels uneasy when things are left undone? When there are quarrels? What is your inner emotional life like when you have too much on your plate? This unease and turmoil are indicators of what it is like working in your own strength. The good news is you don't have to do that; God is always offering you His! Create a boundary that helps you unburden yourself by relying on God's strength.

WEEK 24

Seeing What's Really Important

"Jesus withdrew with his disciples to the lake, and a large crowd from Galilee followed. When they heard about all he was doing, many people came to him from Judea, Jerusalem, Idumea, and the regions across the Jordan and around Tyre and Sidon. Because of the crowd he told his disciples to have a small boat ready for him, to keep the people from crowding him."

—MARK 3:7–9

For much of Jesus's ministry, large crowds of thousands of people followed Him, fascinated by the healings, the miracles—and even the free food! Jesus's ministry must have been quite a spectacle in antiquity, when people had so little entertainment compared to today.

Although Jesus had widespread fame and many followers, He was very careful not to let the drama and excitement of it affect Him or the mission God had entrusted Him with. In this respect, Jesus is a model for us and how we need boundaries to keep us levelheaded and focused on God, not the drama, theatrics, and hype that surrounds us daily. Jesus's own boundaries led Him to find solace and time to think when attention and pressure on Him increased. We can benefit from the same kind of boundaries.

We only need to pull out our phone or turn on the TV to realize the overwhelming number of people and ideas lobbying for our attention. We need boundaries to help us remember who we are, and who God is with us, to stand strong in the face of millions of people, companies, and ideas that want our attention and allegiance.

Jesus understood His mission was to save humanity while teaching the world about His coming kingdom. What the world finds interesting will always shift and change, but the core truth of the Gospel never will. A personal boundary that will help you check yourself and not get caught up in the fads and trends of the day is one way to stay focused on your faith and what is most important.

> **Prayer:** God, it is often confusing to know where truth and wisdom can be found. Help me be more like Jesus and recognize that you are the true way. Help me stand firm in who I am and recognize my identity in you and no one else. Amen.

> **Goal for the Week:** How easily are you affected or swayed by what's going on in the world? Do you place great importance on who you follow, the ideas you believe in, or the causes you support? How do these influences align with your love for God? What would a boundary look like that would help you make God first and foremost in your life, over hype and messaging? How do you imagine such a boundary would change how you view the world?

WEEK 25

Put Your Own Oxygen Mask on First

"The second is this: 'Love your neighbor as yourself.' There is no commandment greater than these."

—MARK 12:31

If you have ever flown on an airplane, you have undoubtedly heard the flight attendant explain that oxygen masks will drop down if there is trouble with the plane, and you should put your own mask on first, before helping others. They say this because so many good-hearted people will try to save the companion next to them before they take care of themselves, putting both at risk. But to help the person next to you, you first must be equipped to help them; you need your own oxygen.

If you don't pay close attention to Jesus's words here in Mark 12:31, you could miss a key idea. It is very obvious that Jesus is calling us to love our neighbor, but the love for our neighbor can only be compared to how we love ourselves. In other words, the love we have for ourselves is an active ingredient in loving our neighbor.

If God didn't want us to tend to ourselves, there would have been no need to include "as yourself" in this commandment. Loving and caring for ourselves enables us to love and care for others.

That is why it is imperative to create a boundary in our lives that leads us to loving ourselves first, and that only this enables us to love our neighbor. Love is important to God. He formed us out of His never-ending love, and He wants us to keep operating that way. It is His love that enables us to love our neighbor as ourselves.

> **Prayer:** God, having a life rooted in your love is fuel for me and what I need to serve in your name. Please help me attach to your love more and more, and allow it to be the agent that catapults me to love all people as myself. Amen.

> **Goal for the Week:** God wants us to love our neighbors as ourselves, but we first must love ourselves. How well do you currently love yourself? How much does God's love for you drive your actions and your very being? How could embracing more self-love enable you to show more love to others? What does it tell you about God that He wants you to love yourself? Take time to reflect and create a self-love boundary that helps you love yourself better so you can love others.

WEEK 26

The Call Not to Worry

"If that is how God clothes the grass of the field, which is here today and tomorrow is thrown into the fire, will he not much more clothe you—you of little faith? So do not worry, saying, 'What shall we eat?' or 'What shall we drink?' or 'What shall we wear?' For the pagans run after all these things, and your heavenly Father knows that you need them. But seek first his kingdom and his righteousness, and all these things will be given to you as well."

—MATTHEW 6:30–33

Worrying can become a way of life. Whether you worry a little or a lot, Jesus has quite a bit to say about worrying. And . . . just a heads up, He didn't approve of it! This isn't because Jesus judged others for worrying. Rather, Jesus saw the heart of the problem behind worrying, which is not fully trusting and recognizing how God provides for us. That's why we need to create boundaries that limit the effect of worry in our lives.

When we truly recognize that God provides for us at all times, there is no need to worry. We can trust and rest in God's plan for the future, knowing that everything we desire may or may not play out the way we hope—but will play out as God wants for us. That is why Jesus says to seek first God's kingdom and righteousness, and everything else will be put in its proper place.

Worrying leads us to self-reliance and self-dependence, which can create a wedge between us and God as we forget how much we need Him. Jesus is calling each of us to take a bold step in following Him: To lay down worry and recognize that God is here with us in every moment. He is all we could ever need, which is why boundaries about worry in our lives are important. If worry is left unchecked, it can rob us of the peace that comes from depending on God.

> **Prayer:** God, thank you for tending to my emotional state so fully that you call me to lay down worry and pick up dependence on you. I want to rid my life of any unnecessary worry and replace it with bold trust in you, but I need your help to show me how you will fill the gaps so I can walk away from worrying. Amen.

> **Goal for the Week:** Has worrying ever brought good to your life? Try to recall moments when you have worried—what did it actually accomplish? It's hard to worry and rest in the Lord at the same time. Has your worrying ever caused friction between your rest in God and the problem you are worrying about? Spend some time really thinking about the fruit of worrying and what could replace worrying when you are afraid. When you have the answer, create a boundary for taming worry in your life to enable you to embrace rest and trust that God provides.

Check In with the Lord

You're halfway through a year of exploring healthy Christian boundaries, and it's time to again stop and reflect on what you have learned and ask yourself how you are changing. How has God been stirring in your heart over the past 26 weeks?

How has implementing boundaries affected your joy and happiness? How would you describe your current state of emotional and spiritual health? Where are the areas where you feel boundaries have most eased your day-to-day challenges?

What has been the greatest benefit of thinking about and implementing boundaries in your life? How has your relationship with God changed or grown as a result of adding more boundaries to your life?

_____

_____

_____

_____

_____

_____

_____

_____

_____

_____

WEEK 27

Procrastination

"Therefore do not worry about tomorrow, for tomorrow will worry about itself. Each day has enough trouble of its own."

—MATTHEW 6:34

Have you ever found yourself in trouble because you simply ran out of time? How often has this happened because you just put off dealing with something until the last minute?

Jesus calls us to this very moment, to attend to the tasks at hand. There is a time for everything in our lives, and when we are balanced, we can find the time and energy to be purposeful and meet our obligations. We all have many responsibilities in each day, but we make life more difficult when we put things off because we don't feel like doing them today. I know sometimes we're just exhausted, but many times, the root of procrastination is a lack of discipline—and I say this as a person who used to almost always default to procrastination!

Create a boundary that states you will not worry about a future you can't control, but instead will focus on handling the issues of the day that you can affect positively. Doing so will enable you to take the wisdom of Jesus in this week's Scripture and fuse it into how you approach everyday life.

When Jesus tells us to not worry about tomorrow because today has enough trouble of its own, He is sharing invaluable wisdom about how to handle our responsibilities. We cannot control tomorrow, but we can shape it. If we put off the things that need to be done today, we know for certain that tomorrow's load will be too much for us, because it will have double the responsibilities.

Prayer: Lord, please help me face each day's responsibilities in your strength and endurance. Help me be accountable for my decisions and actions. I do not know what tomorrow brings, but you do. Allow me to find both comfort and perseverance in this reality. I want to lay down my way of doing things and pick up yours. Amen.

Goal for the Week: Evaluate how you use your time to meet your responsibilities. Do you find that you are always running late or are behind on tasks? Do you often feel overwhelmed by all that needs to be done? Take hold of Jesus's words that today has enough trouble, and imagine facing each task before you head on, day by day. If you realize you are someone who procrastinates, create a boundary that will help you take on each day's duties as they need to be dealt with.

WEEK 28

Dealing with Difficult People

"They arrived again in Jerusalem, and while Jesus was walking in the temple courts, the chief priests, the teachers of the law and the elders came to him. 'By what authority are you doing these things?' they asked. 'And who gave you authority to do this?'"

—MARK 11:27–28

A large portion of Jesus's ministry was spent dealing with difficult people. Jesus always seemed to have a naysayer or a challenger lurking around. We, too, will interact with difficult people throughout our entire lives. They show up in our families, at work, at social gatherings, even at church.

When we look to how Jesus dealt with difficult people, we see a common theme: He wasn't stopped by what they thought or did. Sometimes Jesus confronted them and sometimes He ignored them, but He never let other people shake Him.

How did He do this? Jesus knew who He was, and what others said or did couldn't change that. Jesus didn't get caught up in their drama, He didn't feel the need to justify or explain himself, and He didn't dwell on what others said or did. He simply answered their questions and moved on.

Difficult people are everywhere, so we must learn how to navigate them as Jesus did—by creating a boundary to help us. We can answer their questions and move on without any further worry. No matter what it is that makes them difficult, the point is not to try to change them—because we can't change anyone. And if we can't change them, the only thing we can do is change our interactions with them.

> **Prayer:** God, I want to be more like Jesus when dealing with difficult people. I want to stand on solid ground and not lose my footing. I need your voice to be louder than naysayers and challengers in my life. Help me develop an ear to hear your words over me instead of the words of others. Amen.

> **Goal for the Week:** Think about difficult people in your life, both past and present. What makes them difficult for you? How do you feel around them? Do you find yourself avoiding them, challenging them, trying to change them, or being shaped by them? Do you like your current response and is it in line with Jesus's? Take all of your reflections and come up with a boundary you can create that will help you respond to difficult people as Jesus did.

WEEK 29

Handling Criticism

"At that time Jesus went through the grainfields on the Sabbath. His disciples were hungry and began to pick some heads of grain and eat them. When the Pharisees saw this, they said to him, 'Look! Your disciples are doing what is unlawful on the Sabbath.'"

—MATTHEW 12:1–2

Criticism can really sting sometimes. Have you ever done, worn, or made something that received unexpected criticism? It can be hard to recover from. That's why it's important to create boundaries regarding how we respond to criticism—before we hear it, because we never know when it will be handed out.

Jesus was constantly criticized. He would simply go about His business, and criticism would come flying His way. You can see one example in the Scripture for this week. It seemed like the religious leaders followed Jesus only to criticize Him. Can you imagine walking around with a whole group of people criticizing you simply for being you?

You probably can imagine it, because we have another term for them today: internet trolls. So many people have social media accounts where they publicly post about their life; when unwanted critiques show up seemingly out of nowhere, they can be really hurtful. Sometimes these internet trolls will scout out people they don't even know to attack, commenting on every post just to be hurtful. It is very much like what the Pharisees did to Jesus in His day.

Whether you are facing criticism from anonymous people online or from people in real life, you can't avoid it. All you can do is shape your response. You have no control over what people think about you—and it doesn't really matter. As children of God, what God thinks about us is what matters. This is the boundary we can set for ourselves—to handle criticism the way Jesus did. Jesus didn't let the criticism bother Him because He knew who He was. Jesus grounded Himself in the words of His Father, not in the words of others.

> **Prayer:** Lord, let me walk in the footsteps of Jesus and handle criticism as He did. I want to be unshakable in my identity of who you say I am—your beloved child. Please help me be wise and strong when criticism comes my way. Amen.

> **Goal for the Week:** How do you currently handle criticism? Does it make you feel insecure? Does it make you mad? Does it make you obsess about what you might have done wrong? Or do you immediately accept (and agree with) whatever criticism comes your way? Having a healthy approach to criticism is a challenge for many people. If you are unhappy about how you respond to criticism, create a boundary for your life that is in line with how Jesus handled criticism. For example, "When someone criticizes me, I will turn to God immediately and ask Him to help me evaluate and process it."

WEEK 30

Don't Be Too Quick to Respond

"Better a patient person than a warrior, one with self-control than one who takes a city."

—PROVERBS 16:32

Have you ever overreacted or said something you wished you could take back? Of course you have! We have all done that. Everyone has said things in a moment of anger or fear or defensiveness that we wish we could take back. That is why this proverb is so important for us: it speaks directly to reacting without stopping to think. So many problems, misunderstandings, and pain could be avoided if we all would just pause before responding—in person or on the internet.

We often become embroiled in an argument simply because we didn't take time to breathe and cool down. Taking time out and stepping away from a situation can bring so much clarity and peace, and it helps us make a wiser and more Christlike response. We need time to process the situation and our emotions. When we are able to create a little space between our interactions, we set ourselves up for more success, even in a conflict.

This space we create can be best spent as time with God, going over the situation and seeking His remedy. If you can make this a firm boundary—take a breath and turn to God—it will help dramatically de-escalate issues. God's way is often found when we connect with Him over specific issues and problems. This is why it's important not to be too quick to respond: You give yourself time to let God shape your response.

> **Prayer:** God, help me take a deep breath before responding in a heated moment or a problematic situation. I want to run to you instead of defending my point of view or expressing my anger. Help me create a good boundary to lean on you as I face hardships with others. Amen.

> **Goal for the Week:** Recall any time in the past when you wish you could have taken back what you said or did. Try to step into all the emotions and actions of your reaction, because they will help shape your boundary for this week. If you could have done things differently, what would you have done? Take all of this and forge a boundary that will help you combat responding in anger without taking a breath and turning to God. Will your boundary consist of connecting to God and seeking His way before you respond to future problems and conflicts? Consider all of this as you create this week's boundary.

WEEK 31

How to Stick to Your Guns

"Trust in the Lord with all your heart and lean not on your own understanding; in all your ways submit to him, and he will make your paths straight."

—**PROVERBS 3:5–6**

Have you ever finally made up your mind about a difficult decision, then spoken to someone who tried to talk you out of your choice? I'm not speaking about choices that are harmful, but rather the decision you've prayerfully and methodically pondered with God, only to find that the first person you share it with immediately offers a different suggestion.

It can be confusing and downright frustrating when people challenge our decisions and, even worse, try to change our minds. There will always be people who want us to follow their ideas of what we should do in our families, workplace, and with others. There are just some people who chronically want their own way or think they know what's best for everyone.

Engaging with people who challenge your calling can be difficult. One way to combat this is by creating a boundary about decision-making in and through the Lord. This week's Scripture shows how we can find confidence that God is the one who provides clarity for our path, and it's only by following and depending on the Lord that we truly find our way forward.

God will reveal wisdom and guidance to you as long as you seek Him and continue to ask Him to make your paths straight. When you do this, you will gain the confidence to be able to stick to your guns and not allow others to change your mind, because you know God put you on your path.

> **Prayer:** God, I want your guidance and direction in my decision-making. From big to small decisions, I want you to shape them and help me find the right path. When others try to sway me from doing what you helped me decide, help me stand strong in my decision, knowing you are behind it. Amen.

> **Goal for the Week:** Try to recall a time you made up your mind about something and felt good about it, until you talked to someone who unraveled your resolve. What was that like? Did you regret following their advice or was it helpful? Now think about how often you consult God when making decisions. On a scale from 1 to 10, how often do you depend on the Lord when making decisions? Do you think if you made decisions with God's guidance that you would feel more confident in your decision-making and others wouldn't be able to change your mind? What boundary could you create to reinforce this?

WEEK 32

Let Others Also Take Responsibility

"Moses's father-in-law replied, 'What you are doing is not good. You and these people who come to you will only wear yourselves out. The work is too heavy for you; you cannot handle it alone.'"

—EXODUS 18:17–18

Do you ever feel like you're the only one who cares or is making any attempt to lead? Carrying burdens alone often leads to personal chaos and low morale. You see this happen in church, when one person shoulders an entire ministry or event because there seems to be no one else to help. You can also see this in families when one person disproportionately carries the bulk of the labor. Many giving and good-natured people face this problem daily because they always want to help.

Yes, we can do a lot from our own strength, carry much personal responsibility, and get a lot done by ourselves. But within systems like churches, families, relationships, and even workplaces, we must learn to lean on others to help shoulder the burden.

There is wisdom in Jethro's words to Moses that he is working too hard and doing too much. Moses was settling every dispute within the tribe and was so overwhelmed with these conflicts that he couldn't get anything else done. If this sounds familiar, you need to delegate and cut back your workload so you can have a greater impact through smart use of your time. Just because you can do something by yourself without help doesn't mean you should.

After Jethro's warning about taking on too much, Moses created a system of judges. We, too, can create a boundary to help us lighten the load we carry by inviting others to help shoulder the responsibility. God doesn't want us to work all on our own; it isn't good for us. That's why we need a boundary to seek help before we become overwhelmed.

> **Prayer:** God, please reveal and bring forth people who can help me with the responsibilities I have. Help me see that I can't do this all on my own, and open my eyes to see people who can help. Amen.

> **Goal for the Week:** Do you get overwhelmed, exhausted, and worried when dealing with a big project or a specific responsibility? Do you find that you carry a lot of the burden, if not all of the burden, because no one else is jumping in to help? What would it look like if more people did help? Assess all these feelings and bring them before the Lord, asking Him what He thinks about your actions and feelings. After some prayer and journaling time, come up with a way to follow Jethro's advice in your own life by creating a boundary that sets you to seek more help when you need it.

WEEK 33

Is the Argument Worth It?

"My dear brothers and sisters, take note of this: Everyone should be quick to listen, slow to speak and slow to become angry."

—JAMES 1:19

Conflicts are avoidable; it's always up to us if we decide to engage in the fight. But it takes tremendous self-control, which is a fruit of the Spirit, to walk away from an argument or dispute. I don't mean walk away every time; Jesus disputed with the religious leaders and even reprimanded His own disciples, but there were also many times when He walked away rather than engage in conflict.

Sometimes justice needs to be spoken for, and wrongs should always be righted. But we can't address everything, nor is it good for us to do so. As Christians, we must depend on God as our source of strength and guidance to know when to engage in a conflict and when to simply walk away. We will always face conflict in our lives, because having relationships with others is never an easy thing. Relationships are messy and hard, but they can also be very rewarding and good. But if we are always engaged in conflict with others, will that lead to a more joyous and peaceful life?

This is why James calls for all Christians to be slow to speak and slow to become angry, defaulting to listening rather than talking or defending. Jesus modeled this throughout His entire ministry, and we should too—after all, Jesus's way is what we're seeking.

When confronted with another potential conflict in your life, ask yourself: Is the argument worth it? Will it lead you on the road you want to be on, or further from it? Your answer will determine whether you need a boundary in this area.

> **Prayer:** God, help me see when to engage in a dispute and when to remain silent, quick to listen and slow to anger. I want my life to glorify you, and if I am always in conflict, how will I find peace and joy? Help me choose your strength and your way, especially when conflicts arise. Amen.

> **Goal for the Week:** Evaluate how often you are slow to speak and slow to become angry. How well do you follow the advice in James 1:19? If you were slower to anger and slower to speak, do you think you would experience less conflict? Think about how God wants you to handle conflict and arguments. What would it look like for you to handle conflict the way Jesus did? Remember, Jesus did have disputes, but He didn't engage in every argument, and was fully in control of His emotions and did not sin. Spend some time in prayerful reflection and forge a boundary that includes James 1:19 in your life.

WEEK 34

Identifying Your Triggers

"No temptation has overtaken you except what is common to mankind. And God is faithful; He will not let you be tempted beyond what you can bear. But when you are tempted, He will also provide a way out so that you can endure it."

—**1 CORINTHIANS 10:13**

It took me a while to understand my own triggers, because I didn't consciously notice how I responded when I talked to a certain person in my life. I would be in a tailspin after conversations with them, in shock at what they said to me, and hurting immensely from the relationship. It wasn't until my husband pointed out that I needed to set a boundary on when I would talk to this person that I understood how unhealthy the relationship was and things began to improve. I didn't see the pattern because I was in it too long. But once I saw that I was triggered by this person, I knew I needed to be strategic in my relationship with them going forward.

Do you know what your buttons are? Do you know what sets you off? It's important to understand what triggers you have that will send you into a downward spiral. You need to be consciously aware of the things that are leading you to unhappiness and that may be toxic in your life. Then set a very important boundary in your life to limit or be strategic in your interaction with people or things that bring on loads of anxiety, anger, fear, or depression.

I want to be very clear that this isn't avoidance, but rather a way to become healthier and stronger while understanding yourself better. The goal is to limit or prevent situations that will cause you trauma. As Paul reminds us, the Lord will help you through all of this and will never give you more than you can endure. Take comfort and strength from the verse for this week and allow it to shape your boundary.

> **Prayer:** Lord, you know me so well; you know where my weaknesses are and what my potential is. I thank you for your endless love, and I ask you to help me better understand what sets me off and what's harmful in my life. Illuminate things that need to be limited or eliminated so your peace can permeate my life. Amen.

> **Goal for the Week:** While inviting God into your reflection, think back to some times in your life when a conversation or situation left you rattled for days. What happened, and has this repeated itself in your life at other times? Is there a correlation or connection point among these scenarios? Can you identify patterns you could change and triggers to avoid? What kind of boundaries can you create to help avoid situations that trigger negativity within you?

WEEK 35

You Are Only Responsible for Yourself

"Each one should test their own actions. Then they can take pride in themselves alone, without comparing themselves to someone else, for each one should carry their own load."

—GALATIANS 6:4–5

Have you ever felt responsible for the feelings or actions of another? Relationships are complex and deep and can entangle us in ways we're often not aware of. In long-lasting and close relationships, like with family members or a romantic relationship, we can often take on the other person's feelings and begin to believe we are responsible for their emotional well-being.

But we are not called to this, because we are responsible for no one but ourselves. Instead, our call is to walk closely with God and to choose to follow His will. When our words and actions are aligned with the will of God, we have nothing to fear, nor do we bear responsibility for what others will do—which is beyond our control.

That said, sometimes big-hearted people have a very hard time separating their feelings of responsibility from those they love. Many will stay in jobs and even relationships they don't want to be in because they're afraid of what will happen to others if they leave. Essentially, they become trapped. This is why Paul writes in Galatians that every person should carry their own load.

There is a difference between sympathizing with someone you love and taking on their problems. When you become entangled in the emotional states of others, it takes a toll on your own life. Only God can handle that kind of load, and He knows that you're incapable of carrying that responsibility. If you find yourself in the predicament of carrying the burdens of others, you might need to set a boundary in your life about how deeply you get involved in other people's problems.

> **Prayer:** God, help me see the line between caring for and being emotionally over-invested in people. I want to help others, especially those I love, but I want to be healthy and not take on their emotions. Help me find this line and trust in your providence over the situation. Amen.

> **Goal for the Week:** Evaluate how you respond when people you love have issues. Does caring for and loving others mean taking on their problems emotionally in a way that starts to affect your well-being or preoccupy your mind? What might be the issue with taking on others' problems? Do you think God is calling you to do this, or is God calling you to help them in another way, such as lifting them up in prayer and being available in a way that doesn't make you vulnerable to taking on too much? What could a boundary look like for you that helps you avoid taking on others' emotional states?

WEEK 36

Meet Problems Proactively

"Diligent hands will rule, but laziness ends in forced labor."

—PROVERBS 12:24

This week's proverb points to the simple reality that we can either take control of our problems or let them take control of us. This is why we need to set boundaries with ourselves to stop avoiding issues, but instead take them on and deal with unpleasant realities as they arise.

Sometimes it's tempting to address an issue only when you are asked to—or when you can't put it off any longer. But if you know that issue has to be dealt with sooner or later, why not sooner, and before it gets worse?

Avoiding problems feels good in the moment, but it's a false comfort that ultimately can undermine your sense of security and well-being, as things pile up and get out of control. You'll find instead that being proactive with challenges is a healthy way to take control, particularly when you know God is by your side. That's why creating boundaries for yourself will gently lead you to take on the challenges of the day, save you from eventually having to deal with a heap of chaos, and free up your energy for more meaningful activities.

A commitment to meeting your problems head-on means looking a step beyond what is right in front of you and anticipating the consequences of both action and inaction. How can you lower your stress and take greater control over the issues you face by being proactive?

> **Prayer:** God, help me become stronger and more capable of dealing with issues as they arise. I trust that you will be with me as I seek to be more proactive in handling problems, and I am eager and excited to see how my space for you grows as my list of problems diminishes. Amen.

> **Goal for the Week:** Where are the areas in your life where you struggle most with being proactive? Are there certain situations or problems you tend to put off? How could being more proactive solve issues you're currently facing? If you were to make a personal boundary that insisted that you become more proactive, what would it look like? How would you hope that boundary can free you to focus on the more important issues in your life?

WEEK 37

Stop Trying to Win People Over

"On the contrary, we speak as those approved by God to be entrusted with the gospel. We are not trying to please people but God, who tests our hearts."

—1 THESSALONIANS 2:4

Have you ever encountered a person who just didn't seem to like you, for no apparent reason? This can be a very unnerving experience and might even cause you to question yourself. But it's also possible that they're just a difficult person; someone harsh and unfriendly. And yet you still have a strong desire to win them over. You might even believe there is a secret formula to get them to like you, if you could just figure it out.

If you're like most people, myself included, at least once in your life you have gone out of your way to extend kindness, offer help, and try to be as friendly as possible, with the idea of winning over someone like this. Perhaps the discomfort of being around someone who doesn't like you is just more than you can bear.

Paul reminds us that our goal should never be pleasing people, but rather pleasing God, who is fair, trustworthy, and wants our love and affection. With this in mind, remember that dealing with a difficult person means one of two options: You can keep striving to win them over, or you can accept that what they think of you doesn't affect your worth.

We need boundaries to remind us how to deal with people who don't like us, because you can't control everything and a difficult person almost certainly has problems with other people. In fact, let's be honest—you're probably just one of many. So commit to building a boundary around trying to win everyone over and instead focus on being pleasing to God.

> **Prayer:** God, help me be comfortable with myself, no matter who I'm around and how they feel about me. Guide me to a deeper understanding that my worth comes from you, not what anyone thinks of me. Help me grow stronger in my resilience and not be overwhelmed by trying to please others. Amen.

> **Goal for the Week:** Assess how you respond to people who don't like you. Reflect on a time when you had to work with or be around someone who didn't like you, and how it made you feel. Did you try to please them, or did you escalate the situation at times? What is the most challenging part of being around someone who doesn't like you? How does it affect your sense of worth? How can you establish boundaries to protect yourself from feeling overwhelmed in this circumstance, and how can a boundary like that help you to be more comfortable in yourself, no matter what?

WEEK 38

Breaking the Cycle

"Create in me a pure heart, O God, and renew a steadfast spirit within me."

—PSALM 51:10

Change is difficult for everyone, even when what we're doing clearly isn't working. We still keep hoping that our plans and ideas will be fruitful, and it can be challenging to stop and realize that a new approach might be needed. It's so easy to fall into patterns of habit that we might miss the fact that we need to reassess what we're doing to get where we want to be.

There's a popular saying that defines insanity as doing the same thing over and over but expecting different results. There is much truth in this concept—we all struggle to break out of patterns that no longer work. We engage in the same arguments, are frustrated by the same tasks, and keep trying to solve the same problems in the same way over and over.

This week's Scripture reminds us that God wants us to have clarity of mind and depend on Him for answers and guidance. If you find yourself constantly falling into the same patterns and mistakes, that's a sign that you may need to establish boundaries about how you deal with recurring and broken issues in your life. God is willing and able to help you grow and change, but if you want to break the cycle, you need to consult Him.

A powerful boundary you may need is to recognize that repeated failures and frustrations require consultation with God and prayerful changes in how you deal with them. Don't fall into the same traps. Rather, seek out the renewal of spirit God has in store for you by leaning on His understanding.

> **Prayer:** God, I ask that you lead me to new answers for the problems I face. Restore my endurance and willingness to solve issues, and fill me with the assurance that you are with me through everything. I trust your guidance and ask that you fill me with your wisdom to move forward. Amen.

> **Goal for the Week:** Commit this week to assessing some of the areas that aren't working in your life, even though you keep trying. How can you create a boundary that leads you to being more willing to try new solutions when broken patterns keep failing? What is the hardest part for you about trying a new solution? How does it make you feel when finding answers takes time, effort, and perhaps uncertainty? How do you hope God can guide you to greater success in trying new solutions to problems?

WEEK 39

Dealing with Harsh Words

"A gentle answer turns away wrath, but a harsh word stirs up anger. The tongue of the wise adorns knowledge, but the mouth of the fool gushes folly."

—PROVERBS 15:1–2

Many people struggle to let go of the emotions that arise when we hear unexpected negative or mean comments. If this sounds like you, believe me, you're not the only one! Negative comments can linger in our minds for days or longer, seemingly taking hold of our entire life.

Yes, it can really hurt when someone throws insults, or is rude, mean, or even just disappointing. But as Proverbs reminds us, negative comments are often a form of foolishness; they fail to bring any worth or life-giving value. Even with this knowledge, though, it can be very hard to move past harsh talk.

In fact, we sometimes continue to give life to an incident by obsessing about it, reliving it over and over, and not letting it fade from our thoughts. We may fan the fire when we share with others what someone said or did to us, and this can quickly devolve into gossip. Looking for validation from others about what was said might feel good in the moment, but prosecuting the wrong may not be what we need. Rather, seek release.

Challenge yourself to examine whether your pattern of dealing with hurts is ultimately robbing you of peace and stealing precious time and energy. Do you need boundaries for how you deal with problems? After an unexpected criticism, do you have a defined process for working through the issue with the Lord, bringing the concern first to Him to help you process your feelings and release the pain? Doing so will lead you closer to Him and further away from the negativity and all the hurt that goes along with it.

> **Prayer:** God, help me remember in moments of harshness and negativity that you are with me and know exactly what is happening. Please help me find your peace and love in these uncomfortable and hurtful moments. I want to experience your comfort and healing. Amen.

> **Goal for the Week:** Evaluate how you typically respond when someone offends you, hurts you, or disappoints you. Do you often find yourself reliving the situation in your mind? Do you repeat the incident to others, not in pursuit of guidance but more as gossip, wanting others to see you as the victim too? How often do you bring God into all of this? Is He part of the healing process, shaping how you move past this grievance? Create a boundary that will help you move on from hurtful incidents in a healthy manner by leaning on God more instead of obsessing about the incident and bringing it to others.

Check In with the Lord

Building a purposeful and intentional life structured with healthy boundaries means also communicating your new perspective to others. Spend time in prayer, bringing before God the topic of communicating boundaries with others. Evaluate with God how well you are communicating your boundaries to others in your life. Of course, not every boundary needs to be shared, but it is often important to let key individuals in your life know that you are taking a new approach to problematic situations.

What boundaries have you shared with others? What boundaries do you need to share with others in specific circumstances? How do you hope others respond to your boundaries, and what do you hope communicating your boundaries to others will help you accomplish in your progress?

_____

_____

_____

_____

_____

_____

_____

_____

_____

_____

WEEK 40

Facing Reality

"If we claim to have fellowship with him and yet walk in the darkness, we lie and do not live out the truth."

—1 JOHN 1:6

I recently provided pastoral counseling to a woman who just couldn't grasp the reality of a relationship she was struggling with. The other person seemed to be angry with her and was clearly limiting their interactions, which bewildered and hurt her. We talked about it for a while, and a light bulb eventually went on. "Oh, that's what he's doing." But then it turned off as she said, "I don't like that. I'm just going to hope that's not the case." She made the choice to ignore what was happening, hoping it would go away and the relationship would just become better on its own.

It isn't necessarily comfortable to face reality, but it is truth, and responding to it appropriately is the healthy way to deal with it. John reminds us that those who follow Jesus must work to leave the darkness and walk with God, where the truth lies. This means not fooling yourself, nor being a pessimist. Problems can only be solved when the true facts are dealt with. If you pay close attention to people, you'll no doubt realize that many people struggle to overcome their challenges because they cannot accept the facts before them. Denial will always lead back to the same mistakes.

Hope is a good thing, but hope should be based in reality. You can't just hope problems will go away or solve themselves, or that people will change their relationship with you just because you want them to! When you're able to face reality, problems do become solvable. This is why creating a boundary for yourself to deal with reality and face problems instead of sweeping them under the rug will, over the long term, cause you far less pain than hoping things will just get better.

> **Prayer:** God, I don't want to sweep issues under the rug. Instead, I long for your truth and your way to permeate every situation I am in. Help me when I'm afraid to deal with reality, giving me your strength and courage to face what I may not want to face. Amen.

> **Goal for the Week:** Ask yourself if there are issues or problems you simply don't want to examine. This might be a difficult exercise, but spend time thinking through areas in your life where you have decided to hope for a different outcome rather than taking it on directly. What kinds of boundaries would help you become more assertive with yourself and others, and take on issues in truth? How can you implement a boundary in an effective way that will lead you to deal with problems more directly?

WEEK 41

Don't Accept Others' Bad Behavior

"Jesus turned and said to Peter, 'Get behind me, Satan! You are a stumbling block to me; you do not have in mind the concerns of God, but merely human concerns.'"

—MATTHEW 16:23

Jesus didn't allow people to act whatever way they wanted in His presence. From periodically calling out the Pharisees because of their hardened and judgmental hearts to examining the agendas of His own disciples, if people were up to no good, Jesus exposed it. Even Peter, one of his closest friends, was put in his place from time to time by Jesus when he went astray.

Many Christians have a limited view of Jesus that sees Him only as a meek lamb. But that image isn't entirely accurate, for Jesus was both a lion and a lamb, powerful and gentle. Jesus's motivation for everything He did was to adhere to the will of His Father. He didn't tolerate injustice and would expose behavior that was damaging and not in line with the character of God. Jesus did not allow people to act wrongly in His presence, either. He would call attention to it, bring His truth to it, shed light on it. Of course, He didn't do this in rage or spite, but in truth and love. He was not afraid of any consequences, because truth, justice, and love were what He valued.

Often it is much easier to let a person who is gossiping, being rude, or even bullying others go unchallenged because it's scary to think of what might happen. But we should never allow others' harmful behaviors go unchecked. That's why we need a boundary about speaking up—not only to protect ourselves from unchallenged wrongful actions, but also to protect others who might not be as able to stand up for justice.

> **Prayer:** Lord, I don't want to be silent when others are being harmful or rude; I want to stand up for your truth and justice. Embolden me in your love so that I can speak up for myself and others who are being mistreated. Amen.

> **Goal for the Week:** Remember situations in your past when someone mistreated you or others. What was that like? Did you speak up? If not, why not? If you did, what happened? How do you feel about injustice and people being treated wrongly? How do you like it when someone is rude or malicious to you? How would you like to respond in future scenarios? Create a boundary that will help you be prepared the next time you encounter someone's bad behavior.

WEEK 42

Online Boundaries

"So in everything, do to others what you would have them do to you, for this sums up the Law and the Prophets."

—MATTHEW 7:12

There is great allure to being anonymous online. It seems as if you can act however you wish, including responding to others in harshness and judgment. Under just about every public online post, you will find a slew of comments offering either support or disdain. Sometimes the arguments in the comments can become so hostile that the comments have to be turned off.

People can be much harsher online than they would ever be in person. This is partly because the threat of arguments spilling over from online into real life is rare. In a sense, the internet is a safe place to say whatever you want with little consequence. However, this also results in people acting wildly inappropriately, with little regard for the effects of their comments.

Just think about this for a moment: Most of us don't act in public the same way we do online. We don't comment on everything, and we are more reserved in our opinions and how we express them. But hidden behind a screen, voices can become bolder. Sometimes people are braver in speaking up against injustice, but other times it is their anger and frustration that is amplified online.

We as Christians need to live to a more rigorous standard—one that would please Christ. We need to treat one another as we want to be treated. That's why it is important to create boundaries in your life that lead you to represent Jesus in all things, and act online as you would in person.

Jesus explained this simple principle to His followers 2,000 years ago, and His words today still apply to our actions online. We are called to a higher standard, one that represents Jesus. How we speak and comment, and even what we view, should all be in line with our Savior's teachings.

> **Prayer:** Jesus, I want to represent you everywhere I go—even online. Please help me be accountable for my actions and interactions online. May I always be cognizant of how I am representing you online, because I want to bring glory to you always. Amen.

> **Goal for the Week:** Review your behavior online and think about whether you are representing Jesus's values and teaching when you use the internet. Do you comment on people's posts with accountability? Are you doing things online that Jesus would approve of? Imagine what it would be like for you to represent Jesus in your actions online. What would that look like for you? Create a boundary that helps you act online in accordance with Jesus's teachings.

WEEK 43

Are You Being Authentic Online?

"But the Lord said to Samuel, 'Do not consider his appearance or his height, for I have rejected him. The Lord does not look at the things people look at. People look at the outward appearance, but the Lord looks at the heart.'"

—1 SAMUEL 16:7

Much has been discussed lately about how some people enhance and/or manipulate their social media profiles. Some spend hours perfecting their photos and are obsessed with how they look online. Gaining more likes and followers is a life goal for some. These painstaking efforts to present an ideal self online result in images that seem perfect but are never vulnerable or authentic. As a result, the people who post them miss out on so much genuine support and wisdom from others. They have buried away their true self and show only a highly polished reflection of who they are—an image they think the world will like.

As we see in the Scripture for this week, when Samuel is looking for the one God has chosen to be king after Saul, he learns that the Lord is not impressed with outward appearances. Rather, God looks at what is on the inside, the heart of the person. The Lord wants us to be real and true to who He created us to be. While it's not necessarily wise to show everything online, it is important that we are willing to be authentic and are not actively creating online versions of ourselves that are simply not real.

You can be yourself online, flaws and all, and you can especially do this with appropriate boundaries. God never wants you to pretend to be something you're not. Instead, He calls you to be who He made you. So be real in Christ, because it's one of the most beautiful things you could ever do.

> **Prayer:** Lord, sometimes it's scary to be my real self because I feel messy and disordered. There are some things about myself that I don't like and I try to hide. But I know there is no hiding with you and you love me perfectly just as I am. Help me be more comfortable with who I am. Amen.

> **Goal for the Week:** Assess your authentic self online. Do you show yourself as you actually are, or are you just portraying an image of yourself? Are there things you intentionally try to hide or compensate for, such as things you don't like about yourself or that you wish were different? Is there a way, with appropriate boundaries, to present yourself more authentically so others in your life can see the deeper you? If so, what kind of boundary will help you present yourself more authentically online as the amazing person God created you to be?

WEEK 44

Workplace Boundaries

"Remember the Sabbath day by keeping it holy. Six days you shall labor and do all your work, but the seventh day is a sabbath to the Lord your God."

—**EXODUS 20:8–10**

Sometimes our work comes home with us when we don't want it to. Emotionally speaking, we can bring a lot of baggage from work right into our home. This affects how we act, and it affects everyone in our family. There may be a conflict at work or a coworker who is rude. Perhaps there is a pressing deadline or a lingering issue that we just can't leave behind. These issues can sometimes creep into our personal life, affecting our moods and those we live with.

There will always be more work to do. If you were to stop and assess all the projects you'd like to accomplish, or problems that need to be addressed, you'd quickly realize you could busy yourself from morning till night, and still find more that needs to be accomplished. Life is potentially endless work, unless you're willing to set aside the time to take a break and reflect. That's why God created the boundary that His people need to rest on the Sabbath. God knew that the burdens we have in this life are never-ending, and that we need to be intentional in our rest. Today, we can embody this principle from the Ten Commandments by creating boundaries that point us to purposefully seek rest—both physical and emotional—from our labor.

The people who live with us and those in our close circle can certainly help us with the work issues we have, but we must learn to lay down those burdens at the end of the workday and surrender to the fact that we can't achieve everything, nor does everything always play out the way we want it to. This kind of rest is a principle Jesus followed, and it is vital for our peace and joy, and the joy of those around us.

> **Prayer:** Jesus, help me surrender at the end of each workday, know I have done enough, and trust that you are ultimately in charge. Allow me to rest in the work that I have accomplished and help me receive your peace and joy as I adopt this new rhythm of life. Amen.

> **Goal for the Week:** Reflect on how often you carry your work problems home with you. Do they affect you emotionally? If so, how? Do they ever affect those you live with? Do people in your life comment on your lack of rest or respite from work? How could creating a boundary help you stop bringing negativity home from work? Assess all of these things and imagine what it might look like to be able to leave work problems at work and enjoy your time off.

WEEK 45

Church Boundaries

"I appeal to you, brothers and sisters, in the name of our Lord Jesus Christ, that all of you agree with one another in what you say and that there be no divisions among you, but that you be perfectly united in mind and thought."

—1 CORINTHIANS 1:10

Unfortunately, churches can sometimes become centers of cliques and conflict—and they always have. It's a sad phenomenon that can be traced to the beginnings of the Church after Christ died and the disciples formed Christian communities. All of Paul's letters in the New Testament address Church issues—mostly fractures, sin, and infighting. Paul had his hands full with these issues. Even though Christians were being persecuted everywhere, Paul's main message to the early believers was to stay true to the Gospel and not pick sides.

Fast-forward 2,000 years and many of these same problems exist in our churches today. People form cliques, pick sides, and create conflict within their church. It happened to Paul and the disciples, and it happens today because humans are messy and relationships are hard. The invaluable wisdom that Jesus, Paul, and the other disciples offered was to be on the side of the Gospel, and this is the boundary that we, as lovers of Christ, need to set.

When conflict enters our churches, we need to stand firm in the Gospel. This is what Jesus always did, as well as Paul. Being on the side of the Gospel helps create a common playing field and helps people to rise above their own wishes or hurts and recall why church even exists in the first place, which is for the Gospel to be known and realized. Conflict will happen in our churches, but we can always choose to be peacemakers and keep pointing to the real reason we're gathered.

> **Prayer:** God, help me always represent the Gospel and to have it as my guiding light. I know the Gospel is why we have the Church, so please help me always protect and uphold your Word and work in this world through my interactions within your Church. Amen.

> **Goal for the Week:** Have there been arguments or factions in your church? What were they like? Did you participate in the division? How do you think Jesus would handle church problems? The next time division or conflicts arise, how do you want to act? Create a boundary that will help you stand firm when arguments or issues arise within your church.

WEEK 46

Be Mindful of What You Consume

"'I have the right to do anything,' you say—but not everything is beneficial. 'I have the right to do anything'—but not everything is constructive."

—1 CORINTHIANS 10:23

Have you ever heard of the saying, "What you consume, consumes you"? There is truth to this pithy phrase because what we put into our minds will shape who we become.

In a world of relative "truth," we must be mindful of what we allow ourselves to consume. As Christians, our allegiance is with God and His way, not the world's. What we read, watch, and participate in affects us, and either brings us closer to or further from God.

The call for all Christians is to rise above the norms of our society and look to God as the arbiter of what is right to consume. It's very important to make a boundary to help protect yourself from being overwhelmed and confused by what you watch, read, and do.

Of course, God provides freedom to do whatever we would like, but as Paul reminds us in this week's Scripture, not everything we choose is good for us. The things we allow our minds to be exposed to may or may not be beneficial and constructive.

They will influence us either way, and can help us on our journey or hinder us.

We live in a world of overstimulation and endless information. Sensationalism is very popular, playing up scandals, outrageous behavior, and sometimes untruths. So often what we read in the media or online is someone's opinion and is created to drive us to click their link and agree with what they say and believe. As Christians, we must be shrewd in what we consume, who we follow, and what we participate in, because it all affects us and our relationship with God.

> **Prayer:** God, help me have the wisdom and discernment to see what I should be engaging with. There are so many competing thoughts and agendas that it can be overwhelming. Help me always keep you as the source of my truth. Amen.

> **Goal for the Week:** Think about the people and institutions you listen to and follow. How much do they represent Jesus's way of life? Are they providing truth, or just fuel to fight with others? Have there been circumstances where your favorite forms of entertainment ended up causing issues for you, either personally or with a loved one? Do you think that creating boundaries in your life to help you more mindfully navigate what you consume would benefit your life? If so, how can you implement such a boundary this week?

WEEK 47

Toxic Relationships

"I urge you, brothers and sisters, to watch out for those who cause divisions and put obstacles in your way that are contrary to the teaching you have learned. Keep away from them. For such people are not serving our Lord Christ, but their own appetites. By smooth talk and flattery they deceive the minds of naive people."

—**ROMANS 16:17–18**

Are there unhealthy relationships in your life—ones that lead to a lot of pain and maybe even some mental health issues, such as anxiety and depression? At some point or another, we all have to deal with toxic relationships in our lives, often through no fault of our own. We often think of romantic relationships turning toxic, but they can also arise in workplaces, churches, schools, with a neighbor, or anywhere.

It is very important to set a clear boundary that any form of abuse is not okay and should be addressed seriously and swiftly. However, not all toxic relationships are abusive—but they still can be incredibly harmful and damaging. That's why it's vital that you create firm boundaries between toxic people and yourself.

Toxic people are typically very broken people, and while God loves them, our job isn't to endure endless suffering at their hands. As Paul teaches us in this week's Scripture, toxic people can be purposefully cruel and work against God and His agenda.

Sometimes you can't avoid a toxic person and the unhealthy relationship they create. Maybe you work with them or live next door. However, you can create a boundary between yourself and a toxic person that dictates that you not engage with them beyond what is necessary.

More importantly, what they say and do to you always needs to be returned to the Lord for Him to help restore and uplift you. God knows that relationships are challenging and you can't always avoid toxic people. But God will be with you, even in those challenging encounters.

> **Prayer:** God, help me identify any toxic relationships in my life and create a boundary to protect myself from any unnecessary pain or suffering. For those who may be toxic in my life, I ask, Lord, that you tend to them and heal them. Thank you for loving me so much and protecting me from harmful relationships. Amen.

> **Goal for the Week:** Spend some time reflecting on the most challenging relationships in your life. Are there regular encounters you have with someone that bring a lot of stress or negativity to your life? What would happen if you minimized or even eliminated encounters with this person? Boundaries are particularly important with toxic people, so spend prayerful time with God processing strategies to reduce the impact these relationships have on your life. What would be the benefits if you were able to minimize the toxic relationships in your life?

WEEK 48

The Damage of Gossip

"A gossip betrays a confidence, but a trustworthy person keeps a secret."

—PROVERBS 11:13

One thing Christians have been jokingly accused of is gossiping in the form of a prayer request or attaching the phrase "bless their heart" to a bit of repeated juicy news. It can be very tempting when someone confides in us to share that information with others, perhaps under the guise of caring, and it may be even more tempting to spread tragic news. But as Christians, we should never look for opportunities to talk about others, beyond sharing information to help or lift up another.

Gossip isn't just damaging to the person being gossiped about. It's also harmful for those who are truly trying to become like Jesus. Gossip places the focus on drama and tragedy, instead of our calling to be agents of hope and joy. Gossip is a trap that holds us back from God's peace—which is why we need to create a boundary to hold the temptation of gossip at bay. It's not always wrong to discuss another person, but our boundaries should lead us to better understand when we are being tempted by gossip and following an unhealthy path of obsession and discussion about someone else. Strong boundaries against gossip will free you to love others better, turning your words more toward encouragement and support of those in need.

Gossip can sometimes make us feel important because we have information others don't have. But we must always check our motivation—why are we sharing this information? It isn't necessarily a bad thing to tell others about someone's difficulty or tragedy. But if we do share, it should truly be as a way of looking out for others, not to just have juicy talking points. Likewise, when we lift others up in prayer publicly, it should always be with the purest of intentions and caution that prayer isn't serving as a covert means of gossip.

> **Prayer:** Lord, help me rid myself of any sinful behavior in sharing information. Help me never to relish in someone else's tragedies or pain. I want to honor you in all that I do. Amen.

> **Goal for the Week:** Spend time assessing the way you view gossip and how you pass on information you know about other people. Do you find it exciting or invigorating to hear the latest dramatic stories? Do you often feel like you just need to tell someone when you learn a new bit of gossip? What is the most damaging aspect of gossip, not just for the person being talked about, but also for those who share the gossip? How would creating boundaries limit the impact of gossip or change the way you approach interacting with information about other people?

WEEK 49

The Complaining Trap

"Do everything without grumbling or arguing..."

—PHILIPPIANS 2:14

There is a very common theme throughout the Bible that tells us God does not care for complaining. In fact, Paul characterized complaining as being as bad as arguing. And if we all think about it, complaining isn't something we like to hear from other people. I have never heard someone be praised for having such a profound and powerful gift of complaining. So why can it be such a struggle to limit it ourselves?

Complaining only highlights problems, but it doesn't point to solutions. And ultimately, it does nothing to bring about transformation or change. Complaining can lead you into isolation if you become fixated only on what you wish were different. Complaining also comes from a narrow perspective that focuses on pain points but doesn't take into account all the other potentially good things that are happening.

The complaining trap is dangerous because it takes your eyes off God as your source for everything and places them on your problems. God is the one who helps you through hardships, and if you are so narrowly focused on your problems then you will have a hard time seeing how God will provide a solution.

Instead of complaining, God calls you to lift your eyes beyond what is bothering you and to be aware of how much He has provided for you. Creating boundaries for yourself that minimize complaining will help you grow in your ability to see with gratefulness and joy how much God has provided.

> **Prayer:** God, sometimes life is difficult and trials can feel overwhelming. At times like these, help me rise above by setting my sights on you and what you are doing in my life. I want to always be grateful for what I have, not focused on what I wish were different or what I hope to have. Please help me lay down any desire to complain. Amen.

> **Goal for the Week:** Evaluate yourself as a complainer and work to create boundaries to minimize or change how complaining functions in your life. Do you tend to find yourself complaining more frequently than you realize? Do you feel better after complaining to others, or worse? Do your complaints also include a desire for solutions, or are they usually just pointing out problems and how you feel about them? If you were to reduce or change how much you complain in your life and be more proactive in implementing solutions, how would your attitude change?

WEEK 50

The Temptation of Instant Gratification

"Therefore, as God's chosen people, holy and dearly loved, clothe yourselves with compassion, kindness, humility, gentleness, and patience."

—COLOSSIANS 3:12

From online streaming services to same-day delivery, we are living in a society that provides instant gratification. The human capacity to wait for things has drastically decreased as we've learned that virtually everything is available to us at a click of a button. Need groceries delivered in the next hour? There are many services for that! Have a question about anything? Just head to the internet and instantly find endless answers.

While so much is now available so quickly, we have to remember that not everything is instant. For example, earning a college degree takes time, as does advancing in a career. No matter how much technology advances, we are still human beings and have to wait for at least some things. But when we do not have a threshold for waiting, our patience suffers. And patience is something we need if we want to be the kind of well-rounded and whole person Paul describes in this week's Scripture.

When we fail to practice patience, we lose peace and become more irritable. Creating a boundary in your life that states you will not become upset or disheartened when you have to wait patiently is one way to combat the temptations of instant gratification. Patience is, in many ways, like a muscle that needs to be exercised or it will otherwise atrophy. So embrace patience and be willing to find both humility and joy in moments of waiting, knowing God will bless your willingness to wait.

> **Prayer:** Lord, help me embrace patience. The world wants things fast, but I know that some things take time and require patience and endurance. Please magnify these holy virtues in me so that I can have a more peaceful and joyous life. Amen.

> **Goal for the Week:** What are the areas in your life where you most hate waiting? Have you always felt this way, or do you think your lack of patience has grown as time has passed and technology has become a more central part of your life? How could boundaries in your life lead you to having greater patience and seeing hope and joy in waiting? What do you think would be the biggest benefit in your life to this kind of boundary, and how could it change the way you approach each day?

WEEK 51

Avoiding Anger

"Do not be quickly provoked in your spirit, for anger resides in the lap of fools."

—ECCLESIASTES 7:9

Is being angry unbiblical? Anger isn't necessarily sinful, because we see in Scripture both God and Jesus display anger toward injustice. We know that Jesus never sinned and that God is perfect, so when we experience anger we can trust that righteous anger isn't the problem. It's the frequency and quickness of unrighteous anger that is an issue.

Anger isn't often displayed in Scripture, but when it is shown, particularly from Jesus or discussed by early leaders, it should clue us in to when anger might or might not be appropriate. As this week's Scripture teaches us, anger should be very slow to come.

Attempting to will anger away is not healthy. Repressing anger can lead to worse problems and bigger explosions. Processing with a mentor or a counselor why you're angry could be a very good way to temper anger. Dealing with your anger, especially if you get angry frequently, should also be something you take to the Lord and ask Him to help you with.

God is the one who calls us to a life that is peaceful and filled with joy. So if He calls us from anger, He will also enable us to deal with our anger. If you find yourself angry a lot, then create a boundary that can lead you to get extra help with processing your anger, and pray to God to help you find the right tools and resources to conquer unrighteous anger in your life.

> **Prayer:** God, please help me only display righteous anger. I know that you are very slow to anger, and I want to follow in your footsteps and act in accordance with your way. Please help me find resources and people who can help me process my anger when it arises, so I can be in line with your will. Amen.

> **Goal for the Week:** In your mind, what is the difference between sinful anger and righteous anger? What are the warning signs that the anger you're experiencing has moved from a place of justice to one of spite? What is the hardest thing about controlling your anger, or keeping it from becoming destructive or unproductive? How would strong boundaries around self-damaging anger be beneficial to you personally? What are some of the ways you believe you would change for the better if you were to exhibit greater control and boundaries over anger in your life?

WEEK 52

Embody Self-Control

"Rather, he must be hospitable, one who loves what is good, who is self-controlled, upright, holy, and disciplined."

—TITUS 1:8

We finish this book with the call to embody self-control, because what boundaries really are is self-control at work in a variety of ways. It is being wisely self-disciplined in order to have a more harmonious and joyful life. Healthy boundaries enable you to build the kind of life you want, and still respect and love others, especially difficult people. Boundaries also help you step into the way Jesus lived His life, since a major component of Jesus's ministry was practicing self-control.

What Paul is describing in this week's Scripture is the epitome of a Christian leader: someone who exemplifies being Christlike and has a lifestyle of dedication, purpose, and self-control. So many problems in our lives can be dealt with by having good, healthy boundaries and reinforcing them through self-control.

Self-control is being able to say no in the moment in order to get to your goals. It's setting your sights on something bigger and more purposeful than what's tempting you. Self-control is vital for people who are looking to overcome, to change their lives, and to establish new patterns that will ultimately lead them to their goals.

As Christians, we should always be growing and becoming more like Jesus. Jesus practiced self-control often in His ministry, and we have the opportunity to walk in His footsteps by taking on this discipline in our lives. As we walk closer and closer with Him, our lives constantly change for the better—which will lead to great and wonderful things!

Prayer: Jesus, thank you for showing me the way to health and happiness. Thank you for paving a way for me to follow so that I can have a better model for life. I am beyond thankful for the work you have done in me, so please help me continue to follow in your footsteps. Amen.

Goal for the Week: In examining self-control in your life, begin by first asking God to help you develop a greater sense of self-control and to trust that patience will lead to achieving the most valuable, difficult goals in life. Are there some areas of life where it is harder for you to achieve self-control? Why do you think you are better at self-control in some areas than in others? What kind of boundary would help you establish a greater sense of self-control and overcome the issues that cause you the deepest problems?

Check In with the Lord

Being intentional in creating boundaries that lead to more peace, joy, and fulfillment in life can be hard work. What has been the most difficult week (or boundary) for you, and why? How has God shown you the challenges with this boundary? Are there any strategies or additional help that have made this challenge easier?

What boundaries have been surprisingly easy for you to apply in your life? What boundaries have been most surprising in their effectiveness in improving your life? How has your relationship with God grown or changed because of this boundary?

Are there any boundaries you haven't attempted to implement yet, but hope to? Why have you delayed creating these boundaries, and what would it look like to have a plan to begin?

_____
_____
_____
_____
_____
_____
_____
_____

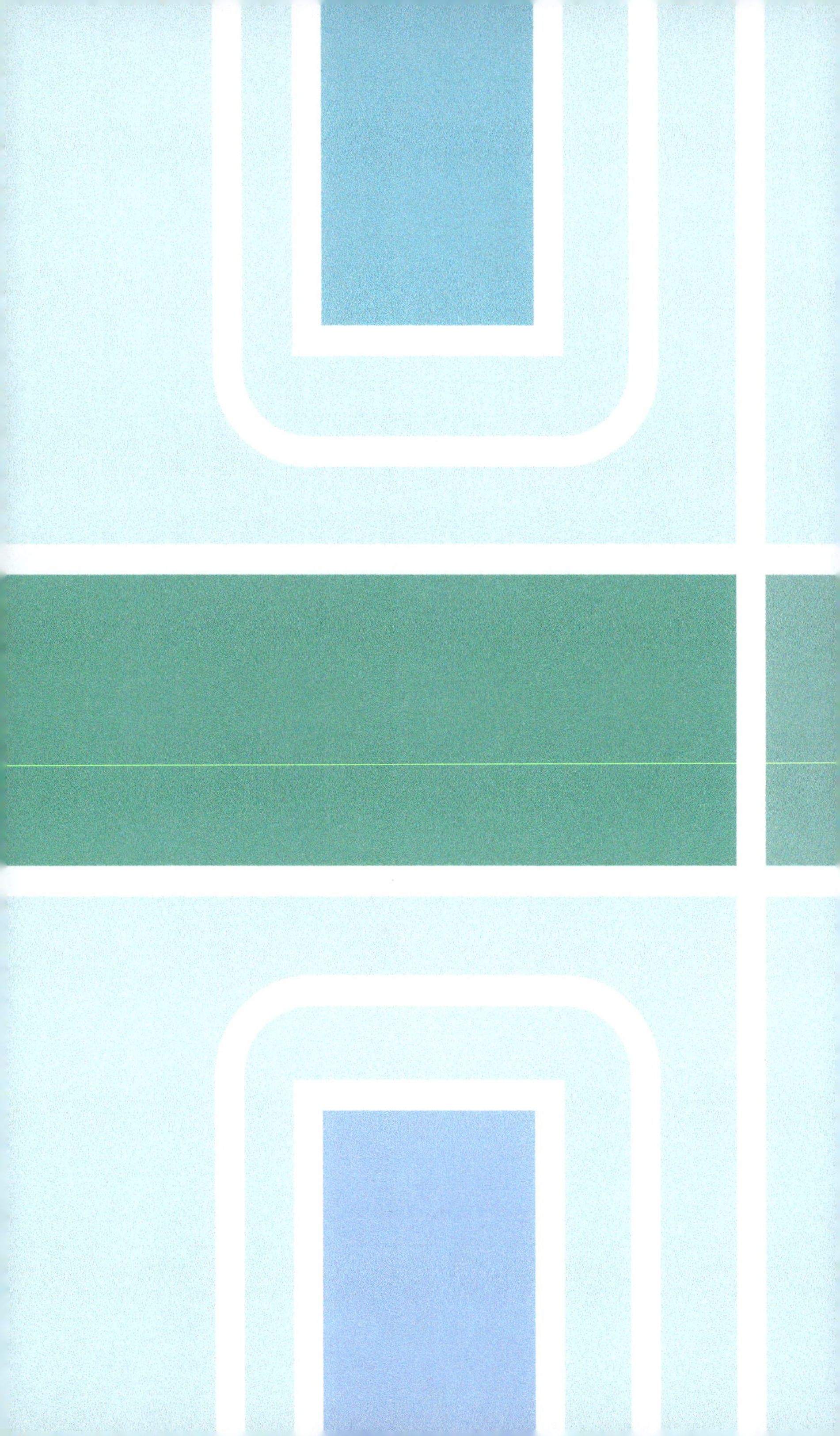

Moving Forward with Your Boundaries

Congratulations on completing a year of rewarding effort in establishing healthy boundaries! You've undoubtedly made big steps forward, but remember that forming and keeping boundaries is an ongoing process that evolves over time as you continue to adapt your boundaries to best suit your needs and desires. However, the Lord will continue to lead you through this process of becoming more healthy and whole, so keep your eyes on Him and allow Him to be your source of strength.

Maintaining boundaries long-term should become easier as you become more experienced in setting and upholding them, although it requires some intentionality on your part. Know that you will face challenges at times in keeping your new boundaries, and that's okay. If one of them comes undone in any way, set aside some time with God to process what happened and ask for more wisdom and discernment to correct the problems at hand. If you keep returning to God and are honest with yourself, you will find the right path that leads to what you have been searching for.

As you move forward, my hope is that your boundaries will allow you to more authentically love and care for others—as well as yourself—freeing you to lead the rich and rewarding life that God is calling you to.

Index

OLD TESTAMENT

Genesis
  4:8, 16
Exodus
  18:17–18, 68
  20:8–10, 94
1 Samuel
  16:7, 92
Psalms
  33:11, 8
  51:10, 80
  139:13–14, 36
Proverbs
  3:5–6, 66
  11:13, 102
  12:24, 76
  15:1–2, 82
  16:32, 64
Ecclesiastes
  3:1–2, 40
  7:9, 108
Isaiah
  41:10, 48
Jeremiah
  29:11, xiv

NEW TESTAMENT

Matthew
  4:12, 34
  5:37, 12
  6:30–33, 54
  6:34, 58
  7:12, 90
  7:24, 26, 6
  12:1–2, 62
  16:23, 88
  17:9, 4
  18:21–22, 24
  20:30–33, 18
Mark
  3:7–9, 50
  6:30–31, 14
  10:27, xiv
  11:27–28, 60
  12:31, 52
Luke
  10:38–42, 38
  18:1, 20
John
  5:6–9, 42
  8:14–18, 26
Romans
  7:15, 44
  16:17–18, 100
1 Corinthians
  1:10, 96
  10:13, 72
  10:23, 98

2 Corinthians
  4:18, 46
Galatians
  1:10, 22
  5:22–23, 2
  6:4–5, 74
Ephesians
  5:15–17, 30
Philippians
  2:14, 104
Colossians
  3:12, 106
1 Thessalonians
  2:4, 78
2 Timothy
  1:7, 10
Titus
  1:8, 110
Hebrews
  10:33–36, 32
James
  1:19, 70
1 John
  1:6, 86

About the Author

Alexis Waid holds a master's degree in Christian Studies from Denver Seminary, where she focused on practical theology and spiritual formation. Alexis has been doing ministry for 20 years and focuses on the human condition and connecting to God for the source of health, guidance, and contentment. She has led countless people online into deeper faith through her website SpirituallyHungry.com. She is a mother of two kids with special needs and a wife to her best friend and ministry partner, Aaron.

CPSIA information can be obtained
at www.ICGtesting.com
Printed in the USA
JSHW021412280322
24320JS00005B/6